Penny Sparke lives in Putney, London. She is married with three small, school-age daughters. After graduating in French from the University of Sussex in 1971 she went on to study and teach the History of Design. She now works as a full-time Senior Tutor in the History of Design at the Royal College of Art in Kensington and has lectured, published and broadcast widely on that subject.

OPTIMA

Childcare Options in the '90s

PENNY SPARKE

An OPTIMA book

First published in Great Britain by Optima in 1993

Copyright © Penny Sparke 1993

The moral right of the author has been asserted.

All rights reserved.
No part of this publication may be reproduced, stored in a retrieval system, or transmitted, in any form or by any means, without the prior permission in writing of the publisher, nor be otherwise circulated in any form of binding or cover other than that in which it is published and without a similar condition including this condition being imposed on the subsequent purchaser.

A CIP catalogue record for this book is available from the British Library.

ISBN 0 356 21020 0

Typeset in Sabon by Leaper & Gard Ltd, Bristol
Printed and bound in Great Britain by
Clays Ltd, St. Ives plc

Optima Books
A Division of
Little, Brown and Company (UK) Limited
165 Great Dover Street
London SE1 4YA

To the memory of Ann Doolan

and for Molly, Nancy and Celia
without whom this could not have been written

Contents

Acknowledgements	ix
Preface	xi
Introduction	1

PART 1   New directions

The new parents	13
The new carers	20

PART 2   Caring in the home

Opting for a nanny	27
Employing a nanny	33
Working together	58
Beyond routine	73
Other options	84

PART 3   Caring outside the home

Opting for a childminder	95
Employing a childminder	108
Working with a childminder	120

PART 4 The day nursery

Assessing the day nursery	129
Council and community nurseries	140
Workplace nurseries	146
Private day nurseries	153

Part 5 Caring for the school child

Out-of-school care	163
The au pair option	177
Conclusion	190
Bibliography	193
Useful addresses	197
Index	202

Acknowledgements

My sincerest thanks go to the following, all of whom have contributed significantly to this book in a number of ways: Julia Barfield, Carole Bateman, A. Beale (The Maternity Alliance), Caroline Boston, Jane Bradish-Ellames, Louise Burton, Samantha Dukes (*The Lady*), Hilary Foakes, Rob Fox, Hilary French, Lisa Harker (Daycare Trust), Sue Hubberstey (*Nursery World*), Miss B. Jefferies (Home Office), Colette Kelleher (Kids' Clubs Network), Denise Lewis, Clare Lovell, Rosemary Parkes (NANN), Dawn Pembroke, John Randall, (Pre-School Playgroups Association), Shirleyanne Seel (NCT), John and Jean Shaw, Mrs Patricia Smail (PANN), John Small, Amanda Smith, Anne Sparke, Jane Stevens, Sherry-Ann Sweeting (NNEB), and Suzette Worden.

Preface

The problem of childcare for all the working parents living in Britain today is, without doubt, one of enormous proportions. In fact, it probably presents most people in this situation with one of the greatest dilemmas that they will ever have to confront as parents. Lack of information, government assistance, and general support and encouragement makes it an area of all working parents' lives which is not easily resolved. Nor is it just a question of financial resources. Of course, money will buy various forms of childcare but it won't help anyone decide whether, say, a nanny will be better for a particular child than a day nursery, or vice versa, nor will it alleviate the guilt a mother feels when 'abandoning' her child in order to return to work.

Across the entire social spectrum, therefore, working parents are on their own where finding and selecting childcare is concerned. Levels of income will, of course, determine the particular options available to a particular family at any one moment but they won't necessarily help people choose between them. Low income families depend either upon government help (which is not very forthcoming), or they have to fend for themselves, which is what happens in the majority of cases. The high level of what is termed informal childcare, which takes place in this country at the moment, bears witness to this fact. Parents, whether dual or single, whose incomes don't allow them to 'buy in' any kind of formal childcare have to make arrangements with family members, friends, neighbours, work colleagues, employers, and other people in the local community to ensure that their children are cared for while they go to work. Often this leads to very complex arrangements and is far from foolproof for all sorts of obvious reasons.

This kind of informal care, which constitutes by far the largest sector of childcare in the country at the moment, is beyond the scope of this book, however. Numerous organisations have taken upon themselves the task of improving childcare conditions in this country and their work will, hopefully, show some results by the end of the decade. This book concentrates, instead, on the options available within the formal sector which are equally complex and hard to decipher. There is no literature available at the moment which covers all these options, from those located within the public sector to those within both the voluntary and the private sectors. Formal childcare crosses these divides in a unique way so that few people have been able to see the full spectrum of possibilities or explain how and where they differ from, or merge with, each other.

This book aims to show the reader just that. Because it is already such an immensely complex subject I have chosen to adopt some strategies of simplification which may, in certain instances, appear to leave things out, or to oversimplify the picture, especially where the question of gender is concerned. I have, for instance, concentrated on the role of the 'mother' rather than the 'father' throughout, aware, though I am, that fathers play an increasingly important role in today's society, both in making childcare decisions and in involving themselves in the childcare process. In addition I have referred to childcarers throughout the book – whether nannies, nursery nurses, childminders, au pairs or others – as 'she'. Once again this is not a true reflection of reality as male nannies and nursery nurses, among others, exist in increasing numbers, especially now that the professionalisation of this work is moving apace. In dealing with the 'child', the most important subject of all in this book, I have used the singular and the masculine almost exclusively. This is for convenience and simplicity only. I could just have well talked about 'children', or the 'female' child. No sexism is intended by any of these simplification strategies.

Lastly, I have only dealt with the idea of the family in the sense of the stereotypical, majority picture of it. I am only too well aware that childcare is even more of a problem for single-parent families (of either sex), and for families with children with special needs, whether mental or physical, than it is for the so-called 'normal' family. Some of the material presented in this book will be relevant to such 'minority' situations; some of it, unfortunately, will not. Inevitably much more work needs to be done before a full enough picture will emerge to take all these situations into account.

Childcare Options in the '90s sets out, therefore, to map as broad a picture of formal childcare choices as it can within these parameters, and with the omissions described above. It is a complex picture but hopefully one which the book will go some way towards helping to clarify and explain and, also, to assisting those who read it in deciding what will be best for them.

Introduction

WORKING MOTHERS

More women, among them large numbers of mothers with children under five, are entering the workforce in the 1990s than ever before. As a 1992 survey indicated, for example, almost half of all the mothers with children under five were either at work or actively seeking work. Whereas back in 1973 seven per cent of mothers with children between the ages of birth and four worked full-time, by 1991 that percentage had risen to thirteen. As fewer and fewer school leavers are currently available to fill new positions and as many women feel the psychological and, perhaps more significantly, financial need to seek paid work outside the home, the idea that 'a mother's place is in the home' is fast becoming a thing of the past. The recession, which has created so much unemployment of late, has not altered this picture significantly. The economic hardship that it has brought with it for so many families means that both partners often have little choice but to go in search of a wage. Simultaneously, increasing numbers of women feel that staying in the home is a restricting option and that working offers them a more fulfilling choice in the long term.

Within both the consumer boom of the late 1980s and

the sharp recession which immediately followed it, therefore, women – mothers among them – have become a vital element within the labour-force and they are unlikely to cease to be so in the foreseeable future. This fact is recognised by contemporary movements, such as the much publicised Opportunity 2000 campaign, which are committed not only to the quantity but also the quality of women's work and which have done important work in bringing to the attention of Britain's top management the fact that employing women has important spin-off implications for the family, not least among them the vital question of childcare.

On a practical level having women as an important element in the workforce means thinking not only about women at work but also about what goes on behind the scenes in their lives. Having children presents women with a set of practical problems where work is concerned, and increasingly these are problems which the employer will have to take on board too. Childbirth, bonding with a young child, the school timetable and children's illnesses are just some of the factors which are usually catered for by women, whether for biological or cultural reasons, and which employers increasingly need to think about as well.

At present, however, in spite of the campaigning work of Opportunity 2000 and of groups like the Working Mothers Association, the reality is that most families, and women in particular, are on their own where these knotty problems are concerned. While legislation moves slowly forward, making statutory and paid maternity leave available in certain circumstances, this only goes a small part of the way towards making the choice of becoming a working mother an easy one.

In Britain today each woman who makes the decision to become a working mother makes it knowing that the problems incurred are essentially hers to solve on her own. Also, and perhaps even more importantly, she knows that she is living in a culture which still fundamentally believes that a young child is best looked after by his own mother and not by a substitute who makes it possible for her to go and earn a living outside the home. In 1987 a British Social Attitudes survey reinforced this with findings that of a group of women questioned 76 per cent thought that mothers should stay at home with their young children. This basic belief is revealed not only by researchers who have interrogated women about this question but also by the minimal number of initiatives made by employers and the state to provide childcare. Compared with a number of other European countries – notably, Denmark, Sweden and France – Great Britain is a long way behind in the childcare stakes and still has a long way to go.

The lack of obvious practical help on offer, and the ideological resistance to the idea of the working mother, means that women who choose this path of action have a doubly difficult task in front of them. Not only do they have to make their own costly, often very complex and time-consuming childcare arrangements, they also have to cope with the high level of guilt engendered in them by the dominant British attitude towards them. It is an unenviable position to be in, therefore, and one which needs all the help, guidance, and encouragement it can get.

Quality in childcare

Once you have decided to adopt the problematic status of a 'working mother', on whatever basis, the inevitable next move involves confronting the problem of childcare. The main question in the minds of everyone who enters into this domain is 'Is my child's development going to be disadvantaged by, or benefit from, his being looked after by somebody else?'. First of all it must be remembered that the majority of children are looked after at some point in their early lives by somebody other than their mother (or father, although it is still a fact of life that it is the mother who is generally thought to be the most important figure in this context). Whether it is a granny, aunt, next-door neighbour or playgroup leader, most under-fives spend some time in the company of other people, even if it is only to let their mothers have a couple of hours off to go to the hairdresser or to the dentist.

The problem then focuses on the question of degree and should be rephrased as 'Will my child be disadvantaged by, or benefit from, being looked after by somebody else for most of the day?'. Every working mother asks herself this question at some time, whether consciously or subconsciously, and is in constant search of answers which might help remove the guilt that she inevitably feels. Current research indicates that there are no clear answers in this area. Although a large-scale piece of research has yet to be completed, projects in the United Kingdom, such as that undertaken by the Thomas Coram Research Unit in London, point to the fact that the diversity within what it calls 'other care' arrangements make it impossible to judge whether one form of care is ultimately more or less desirable than another where a child's development is concerned. This is, in the end, a reassuring result rather than a worrying one because it suggests that the difference, if indeed there is one, is marginal rather than substantial and cannot, therefore, be used as an argument for or against other care.

What this research does indicate, however, is that there is an enormous difference between good and bad childcare, whether 'other' or otherwise, and it goes some way towards establishing objective criteria with which to judge it. While these are probably the same ones as those which sensitive parents arrive at through intuition and common sense, it is interesting to see that research can provide some guidelines in this area.

The key components of 'quality' in this context focus, inevitably, on the question of the children/carer ratio. It is not surprising to discover that the fewer the children, the greater the attention that can be given to the individual child. This is not a criterion, however, which can be isolated from others such as the responsiveness and sensitivity of the carer, which are vital however many children she may be looking after, or the benefits of socialisation which come with children being looked after in a group, however small.

Quality childcare, research indicates, is dependent upon qualities in the carer – qualities which manifest themselves in a multitude of ways in the childcare situation. Does the carer respond to the child's gestures? Play with him? Encourage him to play on his own and with others? Read and talk to him? Cuddle him? Realise that he has on and off days? Understand when he is coming down with a cold? One could go on and on. All these kinds of sensitive responses, and many others as well, help a child to develop intellectually, linguistically, socially and emotionally. In contrast, a demanding or punishing carer can have an adverse effect on a child. Practical things, such as toys appropriate to his age, and a safe and orderly environment are vital to a child's intellectual development, while stability is a key factor where social and emotional development are concerned. While research suggests that the minimum number of childcare changes is desirable, this has to be offset with the other requirements. If problems emerge then, of course, change becomes a necessity.

Perhaps the most sensitive area in the question of mother care versus other care resides in the theory – widespread in the 1950s but not now quite so popular – that in the second six months of his life a child shouldn't have its attachment to its mother disrupted. Work in this area focused on children in hospital and resulted in the beneficial notion of mothers being able to stay in hospital with their young children. Present-day researchers feel that this work laid too much emphasis on the mother as the key figure and that another carer could play the role of the main attachment figure perfectly well in this important developmental stage. What is undisputed, however, is that children experiencing daycare, in a nursery or similar, often demonstrate a higher level of confidence and more sophisticated social skills. This often shows itself to be the case when children enter school alongside others who have been cared for exclusively by their mothers.

For mothers contemplating using some form of childcare for their young children it seems, therefore, that there is no evidence to show that the child's development will suffer in any way as long as the standards of care are monitored regularly and the idea of quality is kept at the forefront of their minds.

Who cares in the 1990s?

Any survey about the nature of childcare in this country today will come to the clear conclusion that the vast majority of children of working mothers are looked after by relatives, friends and neighbours. Much of this is done on an extended family, unpaid, or reciprocal basis and has not changed in many years. For decades members of the extended family and neighbourhood have helped out when a mother has, for whatever reason, had to return to work, and it is unlikely that this will cease altogether in the foreseeable future.

However, with the demise of the extended family in urban and suburban environments, and the death of close communities it is likely that more and more people are already looking for, and through the coming decade will continue to look for, a more professional arrangement with a childcarer. This shift is a fairly recent one for all the reasons that have been outlined already. Society and the powers that be have, however, yet to come fully to terms with it. The traditional 'closed door' approach to everything that goes on inside people's homes where paid work is concerned has also played a part in making the contemporary childcare situation a largely invisible one. In aristocratic households butlers, cooks, and maids were often part of a hidden economy and the sense that what goes on in the private world of domesticity is nobody else's business still lingers on in the late twentieth century.

In the 1990s the world of childcare breaks down into two distinct sectors, however. While the essentially hidden world of home-based care, centred around the nanny, the mother's help and the au pair to some extent, remains outside any form of state legislation, the worlds of the childminder and the pre-school nursery – forms of care located outside the home – are increasingly monitored (largely as a result of the Children Act of 1989) by local government.

These two sectors have, in the past, reflected two different aspects of British society. Whereas the nanny belonged, hitherto, to the world of the upper classes, and has only latterly entered the lower-middle-class household with the advent of the dual-income family, the idea of the childminder has its roots in working-class culture where one woman – usually a mother herself – would look after the children of other working-class mothers who had to return to work. She would do this for payment in her own home. This was largely a question of economic necessity for all the parties involved, whereas the nanny in the upper-class household merely allowed her employer to perform the social rituals that were expected of her. In addition the nanny spared her employer the messier and more exhausting aspects of childcare, as well as performing the somewhat arduous job of instilling in her wards the essentials of good behaviour which were expected of them.

The pre-school nursery entered the childcare scene later. It also represents two worlds: one of privilege and one of need. While today's state-funded nurseries especially cater for the latter, the private nursery focuses on preparing children for school, ensuring that they will have all the skills to make their scholastic achievement as impressive as possible. The trajectory of many upper-class children is still, today, from the protection of nanny to the hot-house of the nursery school.

Today the private, public and, increasingly, the voluntary worlds of childcare have become somewhat mixed together in such a way as, frequently, to conceal their earlier social roots. As this is such a recent occurrence – a product, in fact, of the rapid and dramatic sociological and demographic shifts which have shaken British society over the last 25 years or so – it has yet to be fully recognised and addressed. Books about childcare tend to concentrate either on the more conventional face of the contemporary nanny – seeing her as a kind of extension of the rather stiff, uniformed young woman pushing her perambulator through Kensington Gardens, or preparing tea in the nursery with rebukes about elbows on tables – or on the shocking inadequacies of the state's (or indeed the private sector's) support for childcare for working mothers. Very few texts have successfully combined these different aspects of the same picture.

This book sets out to show how these two worlds no longer exist in complete isolation from each other. Today's working mother, who has sufficient income at her disposal, can choose from a wide spectrum of possibilities as the cost of three children at a childminder's, for instance, or two at a day nursery, may well cost the same as an in-house nanny, and indeed probably more than a shared nanny. The childcare class distinctions of yesteryear have been significantly, although not of course completely, eroded. People who never imagined that they would be employing a nanny, for example, are now finding it to be the most appropriate solution for them.

Today's childcare decisions are increasingly based upon individual situations in relation to hours of work, proximity to extended family, geographical location, number of children in the family, preferences regarding the use of a trained carer or a real mother, size of house, whether or not you live next-door to somebody with a child of the same age etc. There are fewer and fewer rules which depend upon what your parents did before you and very few places to look for examples to follow.

Childcare in Britain in the 1990s is diverse and complex. One woman's solution is another woman's nightmare and once you have made what you feel to be a final decision it will almost certainly need to be revised at least once before your child reaches school age. All this makes the choice available to a new mother a very bewildering one. While much of the choice is made by necessity, the rest is down to preference from what is both available and possible. There are few signs of this complexity vanishing in the near future and new mothers will have to research the full spectrum of possibilities before they make their minds up. Hopefully this book will help to take some of the pain out of that exercise.

PART 1

New directions

The new parents

The question of help with childcare, which has become such a burning issue for so many families in the 1990s, has always been with us in some form or another, although its character has changed significantly in recent years. Long have women depended on other members of their immediate community – relatives, friends, neighbours, younger siblings, and paid helpers among them – to help them look after their young children while they have worked, engaged in various forms of social or leisure activities or simply been unable, whether through illness or some other form of incapacity, to look after their children themselves. Alternatively they belonged to the social class which was used to having help available in the house.

Since the period of industrialisation, however, those sectors of society which have used other people to help them with their childcare have tended to be positioned at the extremes of the spectrum, namely the wealthy and the poor. Members of the aristocracy and upper-middle classes have long employed help in the task of bringing up their children in the form of a nurse or nanny, as she came to be called by the 1920s. As Jonathan Gathorne-Hardy has written in his fascinating book *The Rise and Fall of the*

British Nanny '... the unusual and interesting thing about large segments of English Society, at various times, but particularly from somewhere round the mid nineteenth-century on, has been their willingness to allow other people to bring up their children.' This tendency of the upper classes is rooted in all our minds through such famous historical examples as Winston Churchill and his Nanny Everest and, more recently, through the nannies who have worked for the younger members of the royal household and who have received a considerable amount of media attention. Popular culture recognises this social stereotype, also, as witnessed in the film *Mary Poppins*, and, more recently *The Hand That Rocks the Cradle*.

The poorer, working class has also long depended upon assistance with childcare because working mothers from this sector of society have frequently had to work for money in order to be able to support their households. This presents a very different picture of childcare which is based upon economic necessity rather than social mores, and which illustrates the nature and function of a deprived, rather than a privileged, sector of society.

Today help with childcare still characterises life at both ends of the social spectrum but, increasingly, it encompasses the large sector in the middle as well. Up until about two decades ago it was usual for the middle-class mother to remain at home after the birth of her child and devote herself to its upbringing. This was seen as an important role for mothers in this social class, stemming from the time, in the last century, when the Cult of Domesticity embued that role with a strong moral purpose and cultural resonance. Through this century the middle-class housewife has represented a domestic ideal, linked with ideas about what constitutes a 'proper' upbringing for her children and that of the clean and comfortable home which was thought to be the only place in which to undertake this task.

It wasn't until the early 1970s and the growing impact of the Women's Liberation Movement of those years that the housewife ideal came under threat in a significant way. With the increasing numbers of women from all social classes going into some form of education after school, realising that there was more to life than changing nappies, a shift of female consciousness occurred. The result was that more women entered the workplace (this was especially noticeable in the professions that men had dominated to such a large extent) and sought an alternative path in life to that of becoming a housewife. The new possibility of financial independence and fulfilment through a career in turn caused large numbers of women to rethink the role that having children meant for them. Inevitably many chose, and continue to choose, to juggle work and motherhood, a choice which has major childcare implications.

The new role for many middle-class women in the workplace had a ripple effect upon women as a whole, in terms of their self-image. Even when it was a question of a more menial or less professional job, the importance of economic independence coupled with the high level of socialisation that work brings with it (and which housework frequently prevents, at least in today's fragmented society) meant that more and more working-class women also continued to work before and after having children for reasons other than that of sheer economic necessity. It remained, however, a matter of need in the majority of cases as the importance of 'a home of one's own', and of the material goods within it, meant that two incomes were frequently seen as an essential rather than a luxury.

For a number of complex reasons, therefore, more and more women chose to return to work after having children in the 1970s and 1980s and continue to do so in the 1990s. Many, particularly from the middle classes, also now choose to have children later in their lives, a factor which in turn makes them more likely than ever to go back to work simply because that has become a way of life for them. Statistics bear this out: A General Household Survey taken in 1989 showed that the proportion of women with children aged from birth to five who were in paid employment rose from 24 per cent in 1983 to 36 per cent in 1988 and then to 41 per cent in 1989. In 1992 that figure was said to be 43 per cent. While this figure doesn't differentiate between women who work full-time from those who work part-time, the former rose from 5 per cent of the total in 1983 to 12 per cent in 1989.

Clearly much of the work of women with children at this time was represented by part-time arrangements which, undoubtedly, still relied largely upon family and friends to help out with childcare. That is still the option for many working women who have to rely on informal childcare and who, therefore, have to have enough free time to be able to help out those mothers who have helped them. The number of mothers who work in the home, who share jobs with other people, or who work flexible hours remains high as it is only in those ways that many women who work can manage to cope with having children as well. The large number of mothers in full-time work by the end of the 1980s had a huge significance, however, for the question of paid childcare.

The last significant factor in this picture is the demise of the extended family, especially where middle-class, professional families are concerned. Increasingly people from this background move away from home for their higher education and having broken those roots rarely go 'back home'. This means that the new families which need help with childcare are unlikely to be the ones who have a willing and useful grandma in the wings and who need, therefore, to look for alternative forms of care.

Two fundamental options face the family who has to think about help with childcare in this country: is it to be provided in or out of the home? This choice has a socio-cultural basis to it inasmuch as a working-class family is less likely to feel happy about employing somebody in the home as this would not be part of its own experience. The middle-class family is more likely, on the other hand, to have had some experience of having somebody working in the home, even if it was only a cleaner who came in once a week. Having said that the key shift over the last two decades has been the employment of live-in nannies by families whose own backgrounds were very different, and who were unlikely, a few years ago, to have envisaged the fact that they were going to employ a nanny to look after their children.

This very sudden change is a result of the sociological factors outlined above and the economics of a two-wage professional household which may well be able to afford a nanny (especially the live-in variety) and indeed may have to in order to be able to pay the mortgage and provide its family with what it considers to be the essentials of life. Thus, especially in the suburbs of London, the South of England, and the larger cities and towns of this country, the use of nannies has become a much more universal phenomenon than it was only two decades ago. (Inevitably, rural areas are less affected by this sudden transformation as change is slower there.)

The fact that the new situation is dominated by the upsurge in middle-class private childcare, whether nannies or private nurseries which have increased their numbers dramatically in this period, is due to the relatively poor state provision of childcare in this country. This means that it is less easy for lower income families to have both parents working full-time, than it is for those with a higher income, and, inevitably, the option of part-time help from relatives is far more widespread in this sector. Childminders are, however, more widespread than ever before and provide a means of many women returning to work, at least that is, until they have their second child when the economics involved are not so favourable. The increase, also, in divorce over the last 20 years has added to the need for childcare to allow single-parent families to function. Many women also prefer to work to avoid having to depend upon money provided by the state.

Perhaps the most significant aspect of the new situation in which many more families find help with their childcare than ever before is the gradual change in attitude of the women themselves. Increasingly, as our society defines women more and more by the work they do and tends to dismiss as 'non-work' the task of the housewife (a fallacy which in turn needs addressing), women have found ways of tackling head-on the guilt with which they are inevitably riddled. A number of pressure groups, among them the Working Mothers Association, formed in 1985 and which had been originally conceived by a Clapham-based group of the National Childbirth Trust in 1980, were created to 'promote the value of parents in the workplace and the necessity to cater for their needs'. A gradual shift from the discussion of 'women' in this particular group's literature, to a discussion about 'parents' marks the way in which, in the second half of the 1980s, men were beginning to play a visibly different role within the division of domestic labour and a stronger one in choosing between childcare options.

One of those parents' needs addressed by the association was, of course, childcare and the group recognised as being of vital importance the fact that 'parents need to be confident that their children are well cared for'. Thus a movement was initiated by women themselves to ensure that, if they chose to be working mothers, they could influence employers and society at large to help provide the right conditions for that choice. To this end they have set out to improve the provision of quality childcare. Inevitably this is a middle-class voice but it speaks for working mothers in general.

The changes that have come about within the nature and value systems of family life over the last two decades have yet to be fully digested as they have occurred so quickly. The two-wage family on the scale in which it now exists is a new phenomenon, and today the question of childcare is related almost exclusively to that idea of the 'working mother'. Of course, the aristocratic idea of employing a nanny to perform the less attractive aspects of the work created by the arrival of a baby, and to ensure that the child is taught all its social graces, still exists to a limited extent. It has been significantly overtaken, however, by the need for childcarers to act as mother substitutes in the absence of the mother. The new family situation, in turn, requires a new breed of carers who understand and are responsive to its demands and who can provide the quality childcare that is vital to ensuring that a child's development is not impaired and that working parents, especially mothers, can be confident that their children are being looked after as well as, or ideally better than, they would be if the mothers were performing this task themselves.

The new carers

If, where childcare is concerned, the requirements of many parents have been transformed over the last two decades, the carers whose job it is to fulfil those requirements also belong to a new generation which is characterised by its new attitudes and expectations. Gone, or rather marginalised, is the brisk woman in starched aprons in Kensington Gardens. Lost to history, also, is the bedraggled minder of the last century surrounded by troops of miserable, hungry urchins. In their place is the young professional, trained nursery nurse or nanny, complete with career expectations in front of her, and as happy to work in Surbiton as Belgravia because of the new level of informality and professional respect that can be found there.

There is, of course, still a spectrum of possibilities available where childcarers are concerned – friends, relatives and indeed paid childminders, are untrained but usually experienced by virtue of having seen their own families pass through the necessary developmental stages, supported by as much love, patience and encouragement as it was possible to provide. Today, however, it is increasingly common for childcarers to come armed not so much with experience as with knowledge and expertise.

Just as more and more working mothers go back to work after having children in order to maintain their foothold on the ladder of their various professional careers, so increasing numbers of childcarers see themselves as professionals, serving the needs of small children in a number of situations. If you have opted either for a nanny – whether live-in or daily – or for some form of nursery care – whether state-run, private, community or workplace – then it is likely that your child will be looked after by somebody who has had some form of childcare training. More and more, therefore, at least where the middle-classes are concerned, the working mother/childcarer relationship consists of one professional dealing with another. In many ways, this enhances the possibility of both parties respecting each other and having confidence in each other's abilities. This is not to say that childcare relationships based on family or neighbourhood networks are any less successful, or less founded on trust, but it does mean that the possibility of tensions arising out of areas which are not related directly to the professional tasks at hand can be minimised.

In the 1990s the number of ways in which young women, and indeed men, can become professional childcarers have proliferated in direct response to the expanding need for people with this training, especially in the private sector. The most widespread qualifications (and oldest – established in 1946) in this area are awarded by the NNEB (The Nursery Nurse Examination Board) and consist of a Preliminary Diploma and a Diploma. These enable those who obtain them to 'work competently, safely, and effectively with children aged 0 to 7', and to 'complement the role of the parent/primary care-giver'.

The areas covered by someone who follows the two-year

course leading to a NNEB Diploma include the physical, social and emotional development of children; food and nutrition; health care and first aid; play, language and cognitive development; working with parents and others. The syllabus is geared to giving the young people who choose to study it a rounded picture of childcare. It also includes a certain amount of practical work which students undertake in a number of different locations. The nursery nurses who emerge from the courses are equipped to work within a number of environments, among them: hospitals, where they work alongside doctors and nurses; nurseries of all kinds; nursery schools where they help teachers; and, of course, with families as nannies. NNEB courses are run at local Colleges of Further Education, Sixth Form Colleges and also at a number of fee-paying private colleges. The minimum age for entering such a course is sixteen.

Inevitably newly-qualified nursery nurses and nannies have only a small amount of practical experience under their belts, but they have all the necessary background knowledge to make sense of the experience that they will acquire when they start out on their professional careers. Many such young professionals are keen to have a wide spectrum of different experiences and many will plan to work locally, and then to move on to work away from home, and then even abroad. They often choose to work in both the private and the public sectors as well in order to be able to command an enhanced salary on the basis of the breadth of knowledge and experience that they have acquired. Because they see themselves as professionals, and have definite career expectations, it is unlikely that they will want to stay with one family or nursery for too long. In this respect they differ from the untrained childcarers who are more likely to provide a higher level of continuity. On the other hand they are usually aware that working anywhere for less than a year is not beneficial for them and too disruptive for the child in question.

In addition to the NNEB awards several other forms of childcare qualifications are available to young people who want to go into this particular profession. They include the B. Tec National Diploma in Nursery Nursing; the City and Guilds Family and Community Care Course; the National Association of Maternal and Child Welfare Diploma; the Pre-School Playgroups Association Foundation Course and the National Vocational Qualification in Childcare and Education. The last is a particularly interesting route into professional childcare as it was a latecomer to the scene (launched in 1991) and it is the only one which allows a qualification to be obtained while somebody is already working as a childcarer. Candidates for this are assessed on competence in performing in real work situations.

While the subtlety of relative standards and difference of emphasis within all these different qualifications is clearly important, the sheer number of them indicates the growing need for professional, trained childcarers in the 1990s. The importance of this was reinforced by the formation, in 1982, of PANN – the Professional Association of Nursery Nurses – which is committed to the idea of 'childcare as a vocation, with duties to the community and not simply a job done for a wage'. It is also dedicated to 'the advancement of childcare by study and research', a further reinforcement of the highly professional approach towards this area of work which has dominated it for well over a decade. This represents a complete reversal of the old idea that 'nanny knows best' by dint of years of service and some sort of inner sense.

PANN also plays an important role in setting out guidelines for nannies and nursery nurses regarding their conditions of service. Once again this does away with the idea that labour in the home is hidden labour and sets out visible standards of employment for everybody taking on a job in a private home. While it states that 'this work can be very rewarding because of the individual relationship that can be built up with the children of one family, and also because of the various perks that can often be obtained', it also warns against such obvious pitfalls as long hours, and other forms of possible exploitation. Equally, nursery nurses are provided with a set of professional guidelines 'to promote the physical, social, and emotional and cognitive developments of each individual child and meet their needs within the constraints of the establishment.' The duties and responsibilities of the nursery nurse are outlined as including such tasks as 'to provide a parental model for the child in the absence of the parent or carer'. These guidelines help to consolidate the professionalism of the work involved and the importance of the task in hand.

In the 1990s, therefore, childcare is no longer a question of 'minding' a child in its parents' absence, of making sure, for example, that it is simply fed and kept warm and out of harm's way. Today, care is frequently given in a highly responsible way with all the knowledge needed to make it as effective as possible and of the highest possible quality. It is within this framework, therefore, that many of the decisions concerning what kind of childcare is best for your child can be made.

PART 2

Caring in the home

Opting for a nanny

As we have seen, for financial reasons, many new mothers have no option but to return to their place of work after their statutory paid maternity leave has come to an end. Such leave was set up in the mid-1970s to allow women to have time off, on some pay, before and after childbirth. Although some employers offer better deals than this, by law, providing they have fulfilled the necessary conditions women can be absent from work, and in receipt of statutory maternity pay, for a maximum period of eighteen weeks. They must have worked for the same employers for at least six months by the end of the fifteenth week before baby is due, and must still be in their job in this fifteenth week. This maternity leave includes time taken off before the birth (probably about seven weeks) and after (probably around eleven weeks) the birth of the child. After this period has come to an end, however, they will find themselves without an income of any sort, although if they can afford to do so they are allowed to stay at home up to 29 weeks after the birth of the child and still return to their job.

Other new mothers who are less financially pushed may feel the need to get back to the workplace because a longer period of absence would jeopardise their job in the long-term in one way or another. Yet others just want to get out of the house, see colleagues, leave a screaming baby behind, be able to take a coffee break when they want to, and generally return to normality.

Whatever the reason for returning to work when their child is very young and possibly still being breastfed, this decision means that all mothers who make it will need to think about the best possible scenario to combine their ideal picture of childcare with a price they can afford and with an arrangement which allows them to do their job with as little discomfort as possible. In addition they almost certainly want to participate as much as possible in the care of their child. All these conditions have to be met, to some degree or other, in the choice of childcare that the mother finally makes.

Not many routes are open to her when the baby is very young. Where nursery daycare (provided by the State) is concerned there is less than one place available for every hundred children under three and as places are in such short supply, children with special needs inevitably have a priority. Finding a childminder is a possibility but if the mother is committed to having her baby cared for in his own home and there are no available relatives, friends, or neighbours ready to take on this task, she has no other choice but to employ a nanny in some capacity or other.

The concept of the nanny is, however, a somewhat vague one – the very name derives from a child's term of endearment rather than being an accurate job description. Indeed it can cover a multitude of possibilities from the highly trained young professional woman (and very occasionally man) described in the previous section to somebody without any training but who, for whatever reason, knows how to look after children, to an older woman who has brought up children herself. By far the most common is the first type of nanny who is fast becoming a very popular form of childcarer, especially when the early months of childhood are involved.

In 1980, as we learn from a survey entitled Women and Employment made in that year, four per cent of working women, and six per cent of all women, employed nannies. This shows that, already by then, the majority of nannies in employment were being utilised to fill a gap left in the home when women went back to work. This represented a new direction as up until that time nannies had been primarily a means of wealthy women continuing to pursue a life of leisure after the birth of a child. These percentages have continued to rise significantly over the last decade.

There are now, it is estimated, something in the region of 35,000 nannies working in the United Kingdom, although it is very difficult to get exact figures because it is still in many ways (as with all domestic labour) a 'hidden' profession. There is no local authority register of nannies, as there is of childminders and nurseries, and the fact that many nannies still operate within the black economy – i.e., they pay no taxes or national insurance contributions because their employers would rather pay them the lower cash-in-hand wages – means that it is difficult to know how many there really are.

What is certain, however, is that it is a growing profession even in these days of economic recession. The economic pressures upon increasing numbers of people mean that women's role in the workforce continues to grow and the problem of childcare grows with it. For a two-wage family the convenience of employing a nanny can often make the financial strain worthwhile and it is likely, as a result, that the new nanny will be around for some time to come.

Maternity nurses

One option (although not one which is selected very commonly) of childcare for the new-born baby is the maternity nurse. Help of this kind is usually found with the help of agencies which offer assistance in this area. It is an expensive and, therefore, often considered to be a somewhat luxurious way of easing the burden of caring for a very young baby. If the baby is ill, however, and needs round-the-clock care and attention; if a multiple birth is involved; if the mother is convalescing from a difficult birth, or if there are more very young children in the house, then it could be considered to be more of a necessity.

Many maternity nurses, although by no means all of them, conform to the traditional image of the nanny or nurse, inasmuch as they are frequently older women with a lot of experience of small babies under their belts. Many may indeed have been hospital nurses at some time or another. Also some NNEB nannies become maternity nurses when they have acquired enough experience. They tend to work for intensive periods of time and then have holidays, as being a maternity nurse usually involves long hours, often through the night. It is, however, very well paid (at the time of writing anything up to around £200 a week net).

Maternity nurses, whatever their backgrounds, have usually, then, a level of maturity and confidence which is essential in this context. They are able to reassure an often tearful and post-natal mother that they can take over the task of looking after her baby more than adequately. New mothers, especially first-time-round ones, are often very anxious about their new offspring and reluctant to hand them over to somebody they do not trust completely. The usual tasks of the maternity nurse are to complement

OPTING FOR A NANNY

(rather than entirely to replace) the care of the mother to ensure that the latter can, for example, get a good night's sleep in order to be able to face the day ahead. Such nurses frequently work through the night, therefore, having a bed near to where the baby is sleeping and being available to feed, change and comfort him while his mother is sleeping.

Maternity nurses can be enormous helps to new mothers in other ways as well. When, for example, no grandmother or older relative is near at hand, maternity nurses can educate a new mother in the complex skills of babycare and help give her a level of confidence with which to undertake that task. Unlike most nannies, many maternity nurses have been trained as State Registered Nurses and therefore are able to provide a high level of care where the wellbeing of the baby is concerned. They are usually quick to notice any problems in this area and can both diagnose and treat a number of minor ailments which might be unfamiliar to the mother. Some health insurances help to cover the cost of employing this kind of help which can make it a little easier. If a sick child is involved, then it might well be deemed a necessity by an insurance company.

Sometimes a maternity nurse is employed in addition to a nanny and in these circumstances the tasks involved with caring for the baby, and the new mother, are shared between them. While the nurse will probably work through the night and concentrate on the immediate requirements of the baby, the nanny will take over the daytime caring in addition to carrying out all the necessary nursery duties such as washing the baby's clothes, tidying up and preparing food. Often nannies can feel supernumerary when there is a maternity nurse around, so it is the mother's responsibility to make sure that there is enough complementary work for both of them.

A maternity nurse might well also have a role to play if

a mother has to return very quickly after childbirth to a very stressful job for which she must get a decent night's sleep, or indeed if she, or her partner, need to be away from the house for work purposes. While, therefore, in some ways, the maternity nurse is a kind of left-over from the old days when upper-class mothers felt that changing nappies was not for them, she can in certain circumstances be a necessary, albeit expensive, part of the picture of childcare in the 1990s.

Employing a nanny

Why a nanny?

The decision to employ a nanny to look after your child when you return to work after your maternity leave is based, in the first instance, on two important factors, one financial and the other practical. First of all you have to be able to afford one, and secondly, if you want her to live in your house, you must have room for her. These factors have to be balanced against the more abstract decision of whether or not you want your child to be cared for in a situation which resembles, as nearly as possible, that of the conventional one of the mother and child together in the family home.

In some ways the nanny is the nearest thing to the professional mother substitute (although as we shall see there are fundamental differences in the way each takes on the role of carer) and many of those parents who opt for this formula are prepared to make significant financial sacrifices, and fundamental changes in their domestic arrangements, to make what they consider to be this 'ideal' situation possible. There are obvious other practical advantages as well in having a professional childcarer on the premises: it means less ferrying about; it allows for a little more flexibility where time-keeping is involved; it provides an on-the-spot babysitter; it enables both parents to be away at the same time if work makes this unavoidable; it gives your child a high level of individual attention; and it provides the obvious security of his being cared for in his own home.

For all these and other reasons increasing numbers of people from middle-class, and lower middle-class, backgrounds are now considering the option of a nanny as a form of pre-school childcare. No longer is it the preserve of the upper middle-class or aristocratic family to have somebody in the home who can perform all the duties associated with looking after your child. Although many wealthy families which employ a nanny to make it possible for a non-working mother to join a tennis club, go on shopping trips, and have her weekly facial still exist, this is by no means the dominant picture any longer. Instead, many mothers (and indeed fathers) and nannies work together as a professional team in pursuit of the best possible situation for the child in question. The class differences between employer and employee have been significantly eroded and no longer, in this context, does the old 'mistress/servant' relationship determine communication between them.

In this new situation the question of finances is more crucial, however, as we are not talking about families which have money to throw away. Nonetheless, employing a nanny is still inevitably dependent upon a certain level of income (often from two salaries) as it is undoubtedly the most expensive childcare option available after the maternity nurse. Whether you can afford a nanny or not is entirely dependent on whether or not there is enough money in the domestic kitty to cover all the usually family expenses in addition to paying the nanny's salary (including her tax and insurance), as well as paying for her food and her share of the household bills. Nannies' salaries are, of course, not fixed as they are subject to all the usual shifts in the economy but, at the time of writing, a trained and experienced live-in nanny, working in London, earns something between £120 to £200 net a week. The appropriate tax and insurance (payable by the employer directly to the tax office on a quarterly basis) need to be added to this, as do all the other expenses incurred in having another person living in your house.

It's not a cheap undertaking, but it is one which increasing numbers of professional people feel is just viable, especially as it is not for ever. Many are prepared to sacrifice such expensive purchases as items of household equipment and furniture, clothing and exotic holidays for the period of four or five years in which employing a nanny seems a necessity. It may indeed be the case that one parent's salary is used completely on employing a nanny. This situation, inevitably, only makes sense if that parent is continuing to work for psychological or career reasons, a situation which is not as rare as it may seem. There is also the argument that paying a lot for childcare helps to ease the mother's level of guilt in 'abandoning' her child to someone else.

The question of domestic space is also fundamental to employing a live-in nanny. Live-out nannies (*see* Other options) cost more as they have to cover their own living expenses. It also brings with it all the on-the-spot advantages listed above, although it may introduce the tensions that can result from an 'outsider' living in close proximity with a family. Those tensions can be very real ones if a personality clash develops or if members of the family, or the nanny, don't abide by all the rules of tolerance and generosity which are the necessary prerequisites of communal living. Providing that the personalities involved can find a level of harmony which enables daily life to run smoothly, amicably and, dare I say, enjoyably, another person in the household can be a bonus in many different ways.

A basic prerequisite for every nanny is a room of her own, (preferably with a television in it) big enough to entertain friends in, to sleep, work, read and generally relax in. Professional nannies have most weekends and evenings to themselves and therefore need enough privacy to enjoy their own lives but also enough company from the family to be able to feel part of it and at home. She becomes a kind of big sister in many ways, old enough to lead her own life but young enough to need some security.

Once the decisions about finances and sharing your domestic space have been made it's time to think about making contact with a potential nanny.

Looking for a nanny

There are as many ways of finding a nanny for your new child as there are of cooking an egg. The simplest way – that is, using a professional agency – is, of course, the most expensive, in some cases inordinately so, while do-it-yourself ways – such as advertising in your local newspaper – are cheaper but much more time-consuming. As in any area where human beings are involved, a lot of luck is included in the process of searching for the ideal nanny to suit you and your child's personality and requirements. It may be that your next-door neighbour knows the ideal girl or, if you are unlucky, it may turn out that the most expensive agency just hasn't got the right person on their books at the right moment and you end up paying a lot for second best. No formula promises guaranteed success in this area.

What using an agency does do, of course, is to act as a filter and a protection if things do go wrong. Most have money back arrangements or the promise of a substitute if you are let down suddenly. They also provide both the uninitiated employer and nanny with a level of experience, protecting both parties with their understanding of the standard procedures in this area – among them, for example, going salary rates and acceptable hours of work. They also help the employer by undertaking the initial sift of potential employees. What they cannot guarantee, however, is compatibility of personalities, at least until they get to know you. This can only be judged by the people directly involved. Agencies also ensure that the young women one does interview are at least fully eligible for the job you want them to do.

If for whatever reason you decide to avoid the agencies, you enter a world in which unspoken rules operate and in which you are a complete outsider. You have to be guided by doggedness and a firm commitment to your concept of the ideal nanny. A little bit of research will tell you, quite quickly, that most potential nannies (particularly live-in ones) look for advertisements in *The Lady* or *Nursery World*. The former is a strangely nostalgic periodical which still operates in a by-gone era when household service was the norm for middle-class and upper-class British families, and when the lady of the household didn't soil her hands with work of any kind; the latter, a more up-to-date magazine aimed at the young professional carer of pre-school children.

The next rite of initiation is into the codes which are used in these advertisements and again research is the only way to discover that those jobs which don't offer 'own room with TV' and 'use of a car' are immediately disadvantaged. The ads also offer a perspective on the kinds of salaries offered and the sorts of conditions of work that are clearly expected. One big decision involves choosing whether to opt for the filter provided by having a box number rather than laying oneself open to the mixed blessings of including one's telephone number. While the latter is more direct, it also invites problems. Advertising in this open way means that it can take a considerable amount of time to differentiate between the possible and impossible candidates but with perseverance it can work well. It is probably more advisable to use this route, however, when one has become familiar with the underworld of nanny culture and is in the process of looking for the second, third or fourth employee.

The local paper is a good way of finding a live-out nanny as the agencies and the national press work on the basis of expecting employees to be moving to their new jobs. Many people come from the provinces to London and obviously want live-in positions. People who want to retain their independence and live in their own accommodation will look in local papers, in addition to notices in shop windows, in their search.

Another way of finding a local nanny is to contact a nearby college which runs a relevant course (*see* The new carers) and ask if any new graduates are looking for jobs in the area. These courses turn out their trained graduates in June/July so that is a good time to make contact with somebody who is about to take her first steps into the world of nannying.

There are probably many other ways of finding the perfect nanny for your child, all of which result in successes, failures and compromises. What is most clear about this process, however, from the new employer's perspective, is that the structure is largely a hidden one, passed on by word of mouth rather than by being written down in a book of rules. There are advantages and disadvantages to each route and there is no simple formula for anticipating the amount of money, time and mental anguish that has to be invested in every new search. In the end, though, large numbers of employers and nannies do manage to find each other and form successful relationships which benefit the children in question.

The interview

Interviewing somebody who is possibly to be entrusted with one's child must be one of the most difficult undertakings of one's life. The initial, instinctive reaction to someone's appearance or facial expression can denote a lot: is the interviewee clean and tidy? Does she look cheerful? Does she look energetic? These are the sorts of things that go through a future employer's mind when she is interviewing a potential nanny. Equally the nanny will have similar thoughts and be wondering whether or not this is a household in which she will be happy.

Nannies are best interviewed in the home and preferably by both parents where applicable. Having said that, one must be careful that two people do not overwhelm the candidate and perhaps one parent should take a back seat through some of the interview. All nannies, however they have been contacted, should bring references with them to their interview. This is the only kind of real guarantee that an employer has that a nanny is experienced and that she has the qualities that are needed. A first-time nanny should bring college or work experience references. A nice addition from an experienced nanny is a file of photos of the children she has looked after in the past. All references can be followed up by phone calls as most employers are happy to discuss nannies they have worked with.

It is difficult to legislate about the way a nanny interview should take place because, as in all human situations, personality is so important. At the same time one is looking for a number of specific qualities in the interview – easy-going manner, a caring character, cheerfulness and maturity combined with knowledge about, and experience of, working with young children. The list is endless. As a result one is looking as much at how she responds as at what she says. The child plays an important part in the interview too as it is clear when people are at home with young children, and when they 'have a way' with them. But ultimately, however warm and caring a person is, it's no good unless she is also highly efficient when it comes to children's laundry and food preparation. At the same time possession of the latter skills without the former characteristics is not a formula for success. In the end one is thrown back on to one's instincts and has to trust them to quite a high degree.

The interview is clearly a two-way process though. While you're looking for somebody who will care for your children in the way in which you would like them to be cared, and will be an asset to the household, the interviewee is looking to see whether your approach to childcare is in line with her methods. Are you a disciplinarian? Do you make your children eat their greens? Is TV banned? She is also wondering whether she can lead her life as she likes as part of this household. A chat with the child and a walk round the house and its facilities are an essential part of the interview, as is a description of how you see the daily routine working out. Above all the expected conditions of service and salary on offer should be discussed openly and the nanny should have the opportunity to ask any questions that she might want answered.

Because the interview is more a test of whether certain

personalities are potentially compatible with each other than an examination of the interviewee's skills and knowledge (ideally these should be discussed prior to the interview) it does not need to be a highly formal affair. At the same time excessive casualness will mean that important things will get left out and you'll not be left with enough information with which to come to a decision.

As you'll probably be interviewing a few candidates for your nanny job it's best not to come to a decision on the spot but rather to get in touch as soon as possible once your decision has been made. That gives both parties some time to reflect and weigh up the pros and cons. This is the time to phone up referees and ask them directly what they think. Most will be helpful and can put your mind at rest – or otherwise – if you have niggling doubts. I cannot stress too strongly how much intuition and one's knowledge of human nature play a part in this selection process. You are choosing a professional to do a job for you and inviting somebody to come and live in your home, and getting both bits right is vital.

The contract

As with any professional position, the conditions of service should be clearly laid out before anyone takes it on. Where a live-in nanny is concerned this is equally important although it is sensible not to make this seem like a piece of legislation entered into to protect both parties as this could sow the seeds of distrust from the outset. Rather it is a simple matter of common sense undertaken so that both parties involved start out communicating clearly with each other.

The employment of nannies is frequently done in a notoriously underhand way, as part of the cash-in-hand, hidden economy. This is done for a number of reasons: primarily to tax dodge, but also because many people are terrified by the thought of becoming an employer and having to take on the ensuing paperwork. Neither reason is an adequate one for jeopardising the future of your employee. Without being properly registered as a tax-payer and making national insurance contributions, your nanny is not eligible for sick pay, maternity leave or any of the other forms of protection offered by the state. She is not, in fact, a legally employed person and can never declare her earnings in an open manner for fear of being chased by the taxman. This is not a desirable state of affairs for a young professional starting out on a career and the provision of a contract turns the job into a professional position with appropriate conditions of service attached to it.

Some nanny agencies are very efficient in ensuring that the nannies who pass through their books obtain a contract and some provide a blueprint of one for the employer. While details vary, the main business of a nanny's contract usually includes the salary (net and gross); daily hours; amount of annual holidays (usually twenty working days plus bank holidays); the average weekly number of babysittings expected (usually one or two); whether or not she is ever expected to work weekends; whether or not you are prepared to pay for a pension scheme (if not the nanny is best advised to take out a private one); how much notice is expected (usually a month for both employer and employee); exactly what constitutes nursery duties, for example, caring for the children's clothes, their bedroom, toys and preparing their meals, etc. The blueprint overleaf has been provided as a general guide by the Working Mothers Association – a self-help organisation which provides an informal support system for working mothers through a network of local groups.

Contract of Employment

TERMS & CONDITIONS
It is helpful to recognise that goodwill between all parties involved forms an important part of employment agreements; and where resident employment is concerned, both parties should be ready to accept a degree of flexibility. As required by legislation, set out below are the terms and conditions of employment for the following position.

Name & address of employer

_____

_____

_____

Name and address of employee

_____

_____

_____

Job Title (e.g. 'private nanny')

_____

Date of issue of this contract

_____

Date of commencement of employment

_____

Previous service (if any) counting towards continuous employment.
Job Title

_____

Place of work

_____

©Working Mothers Association
77 Holloway Road, London N7 8JZ
071 700 5771

A blueprint of a nanny contract provided with the kind permission of the Working Mothers Association.

SALARY

£_____ paid in cash / by cheque every _____ day **or** on the last day of the month (delete where appropriate) in arrears and before deduction of Tax & NI. The employer will be responsible for accounting for the employer's and employee's Income Tax and National Insurance contributions, and the employee will be provided with proof of same. NI contributions will/will not be contracted out of SERPS. (Contracting out is only likely to apply if a company pension scheme is operated.)
A salary review will take place on _____ annually.

PROBATIONARY PERIOD

Employment will be confirmed after a probationary period of _____ week/s.

HOURS OF WORK

The nature of employment in a private household makes it difficult to define exact hours of work and free time. It is intended that normal hours of work, for **non-resident care**, will be from _____am to _____pm daily, up to a _____day maximum of _____hours. **Resident care:** hours of work will be from _____am to _____pm daily, up to a weekly maximum of _____hours. Time off will be _____ day/s per week, and/or _____ weekends per month. Included in the maximum number of hours is provision for occasional babysitting. Excepting the aforementioned babysitting, additional payment will be made for any extra hours worked, such as occasional overnight care. Arrangements to work extra hours will be agreed in advance whenever possible.

HOLIDAYS

In addition you will be entitled to _____ week/s paid holiday per year. Holiday time to be arranged with the agreement of the employer. In the first or final year holidays will be paid on a pro rata basis. Paid compensation is not normally given for holidays not actually taken. Holidays may only be carried into the next year with the permission of the employer. You will be free on all bank holidays, or be given a day off in lieu, by agreement.

SICKNESS

Statutory sick pay[1], as stipulated by Government legislation, will be paid. Your qualifying days for SSP will be Monday to Friday. Any additional sickness payment may be made at the discretion of the employer. **Non-resident carer:** every effort should be made to notify employer as soon as possible when you are unavoidably prevented from coming to work.

MATERNITY PAY / LEAVE

Conditions of pay and leave as stipulated by Government legislation will apply. Any additional pay and leave will be at the discretion of the employer.[2]

INSURANCE

Employer is insured against claims for injuries. Carer has the right to see policy. Carer is also advised to be personally covered for claims against 'professional negligence'. Consult, Professional Association of Nursery Nurses, 2 St James' Court, Friar Gate, Derby DE1 1BT. 0332 43029.

TERMINATION OF CONTRACT

In the first year of employment _____ week/s notice is required on either side. Thereafter _____ week/s will be given by either side.

EMPLOYING A NANNY

CONFIDENTIALITY
A condition of employment is that now, and at all times in the future, you will keep secret the affairs and concerns of the household, its transactions and its business.

PENSIONS
The employer does/does not run a pension scheme.

GRIEVANCES
If the employee has any grievance against the employer s/he has the right to seek advice from_____
(Setting out a detailed grievance procedure is beyond the scope of this document. We suggest ACAS as an arbitrator.)

DISCIPLINE
Reasons which might give cause for disciplinary action include:

*Having a disruptive influence on the household.
*Job incompetence.
*Behaviour during or outside working hours prejudicial to the interest or reputation of the employer.
*Unreliable time-keeping or attendance.
*Failure to comply with employer's instructions and procedure.

Should the need for disciplinary action arise, the procedure will be:
Firstly - oral warning
Secondly - written warning
Thirdly - dismissal

Cause for instant dismissal includes:
*Child abuse *Illegal drug taking
*Theft *Fraud *Drunkenness
*Failure to disclose all relevant information at interview

Signed by Employer

Signed by Employee

CONTRACT USERS PLEASE NOTE
This contract is intended for general guidance only and is not a substitute for independent legal advice. In particular it does not in any way exclude the operation of generally applicable employment law, including the law relating to wrongful and unfair dismissal.

FOOTNOTES
Under the Employment Protection (Consolidation) Act 1978 an employee is entitled to one week's notice in the first two years or less of continuous employment and thereafter is entitled to one week's notice for each year of service - up to a maximum of twelve. The employer is entitled to one week's notice regardless of length of service unless otherwise stated in the contract of employment. Apropos hours of work, a Health and Safety Directive from the European Commission is likely to go through this year(1992) leading to 48 hours maximum working week. Consult ACAS as to its implications - 071 388 5100.

[1] Social Security Freefone 0800 393 539 for help with NI, Sick Pay & Maternity Pay.

[2] Factsheets & guidance on maternity rights & benefits from Maternity Alliance, 15 Britannia St, London WC1X. 071 837 1265

For an excellent guide on good employment practices contact Manchester Low Pay Unit, 23 New Mount Street. Manchester M4 4DE.

While these conditions of service are fundamental to the job in question other things should also be settled at an early stage, although they do not necessarily need to be committed to paper. One such detail includes the use or otherwise of a car. Some nannies don't drive at all, others use the employer's car to ferry children around during the day, others are given the use of a car for their private use as well. This should be discussed at interview and agreed upon as suits both parties. Also questions such as whether or not the nanny is expected to eat with the children or the parents is a subject for discussion. Most professional nannies usually eat with the children, letting the parents have a quiet meal together in the evening, but this can vary enormously. Some join family meals at weekends, other don't. This is all down to individual preferences but should certainly be discussed early on as failure to do so can cause misunderstanding and friction. Other minor questions which can become major issues if not faced early on include whether all the nanny's private phone calls should be free; whether friends should be allowed to stay overnight; whether the child should be given food with additives in it; whether he can be given sweets; how much television is acceptable? How long does the nanny envisage staying in the job?

The best possible advice for anybody starting out with a nanny for the first time is to make everything as clear as possible at the outset. Lack of clarification can lead to problems, resentment, to employers getting irritated and to employees getting fed up. Once everything is set out, the chances of a successful partnership in pursuit of the child's wellbeing are considerably stronger. The contract provides the baseline and verbal communication does the rest.

Establishing a routine

It is important that a new nanny learns all that there is to know about the way a household works, and that you learn about the way she likes to do things, as quickly as possible so that a normal routine is rapidly established for the child in question: nothing is more disruptive and unsettling for a small child than change. The first few days of employment are usually spent learning how the various household appliances work; what the child's existing pattern of eating and sleeping consists of; where the nearest park, shops and swimming pool are located, where the neighbouring nannies live and how the local nanny network operates.

This information can be passed on by the employer if she is still on maternity leave, or able to take a day or two off work, or, if this is a nanny change, by overlapping the old and new nannies for a couple of days. In many ways the latter is the more desirable because the new nanny is introduced directly into the complex nanny culture of the locality. This may not, of course, be the case in rural areas where nannies are few and far between but in most metropolitan regions enough nannies exist in close proximity to each other to be able to create a strong support system. This is especially useful in cases of illness when nannies can provide a useful back-up system for each other which makes it unnecessary for the employer to take time off work.

The relationship or new bond between the new nanny and your child needs to be given time to form. As the nanny is most likely to be working, eventually, in a sole charge situation, she needs to be given enough space, from the start, to be able to form a working relationship with the child for whom she is now responsible. This is a difficult time for the mother as she has to withdraw consciously in order to let that new relationship come into being. She is torn between wanting to be the one that her child most wants to be with, and understanding that she will only be able to go to work with peace of mind if she knows that her child trusts and feels close to the nanny and that she has put an adequate substitute in place. At the same time the nanny knows that she has to play that substitute role if her job is going to be bearable and if the child in question is going to accept her as the person who cares for him when his mother leaves for work.

The most difficult time for the mother is when she has to leave for work and physically separate herself from a small child who is determined not to let her go and who is prepared to scream and scream until his wishes are fulfilled. What the mother has to understand – and this is a fundamental necessity for all working mothers – is that the tears are largely crocodile ones. Children understand from a very early age that they can employ emotional blackmail on their guilt-ridden parents to enormous effect. They can also change mood very rapidly and regain their composure before the working parent has reached the end of the street. Nannies know this to be the case through experience and they put up with the hysterics knowing that two minutes later the child will be involved in a game and will have forgotten the parent who has just deserted him, at least that is, until she puts in another appearance later in the day.

For this reason nannies must be given the space to be able to develop their own strategies to cope with this daily situation and to form a relationship with the child which makes it possible to implement them. They achieve this, essentially, by remaining calm through all the hysterics and by waiting to provide the child in question with support and security in its own home. A capable nanny will get a child to wave goodbye to its parents as they leave for work and then quickly provide a series of activities and distractions which mean that he moves quickly into another mode and forgets that he had been abandoned by his parents.

The structure of the day

Each household will make different demands on its resident nanny. Some, where working parents have very demanding jobs with long hours, will expect her to wake the child and give him his breakfast while others will want the hand-over to take place a little later. Whatever the particular circumstances, it is important that the child knows the routine in his own household and that too many alterations to the basic timetable are avoided.

The most stressful point of the day, where the parents are concerned, is leaving for work. It is difficult to avoid the rushing around that usually precedes getting out of the house and this creates a tension which the child picks up all too easily and reacts to by making demands just when they are least wanted. This is where the nanny has to intervene, in as calm a way as possible, in order to provide a distraction which will not make the mother feel that she is unwanted and redundant but at the same time give her the necessary space to get ready for work unhampered.

The nanny's task at moments like these is a very complex one as the relationship – between nanny, parent and child – is a very delicate and totally interdependent one. The nanny has the unenviable responsibility of performing a role which is full of contradictions. She has, for example, to be able to take the place of the parents while not denying them their role. In so doing her emotions have to be carefully controlled as she has to form a close, loving relationship with the child while acknowledging that this must not replace the one between child and parents. It is an emotional situation which demands a great deal of maturity and comprehension on the part of the nanny and the one which probably causes the greatest heartache for all the parties concerned.

Once the dreaded moment of the parents leaving for work is concluded, however, the nanny is left in sole charge to structure the rest of the day up until that second traumatic moment, their return. The ways in which a child is cared for by a nanny in his own home differ from those in which he is cared for by his mother are subtle but worth discussing at some length as they underpin the whole question of why one opts for a nanny as carer. One of the key differences lies in the tasks with which a nanny is entrusted. A mother based at home has a multitude of tasks in front of her at any one time – among them, caring for the child, shopping, washing clothes and bedding, cooking, cleaning, and changing beds. She will probably also find some time for a social life with other mothers, and for trips to the park or swimming pool. The nanny, on the other hand, has only nursery duties to perform, many of which can be done while the child is sleeping, and for the rest of the time she is at the child's exclusive disposal. This immediately puts the child more strongly at the centre of the day's events. In addition, the nanny has less of a sense of frustration about not being able to fulfil necessary tasks, and more energy with which to entertain and stimulate the child.

The implications of these different emphases within the two childcare situations are significant. To begin with a child probably gets more one-to-one attention from the nanny than it would from its mother, and activities such as game-playing and reading books can be given a considerable emphasis. The nanny probably displays greater patience than many mothers would in the same situation as she is not under so much pressure and knows that her working day will come to an end at a specific moment. The mother who stays with her child at home knows that until that child is tucked up in bed at the end of the day (and not always then!) she cannot really put her feet up with a drink and a good book. The nanny, on the other hand, knows that relief is at hand and that she has plenty of time in which to form a relationship with the child and, for example, to relax into games which help extend his imagination.

The other key difference in a nanny's day is the degree of socialisation that usually occurs for the child. In metropolitan areas, especially in London, where significant numbers of nannies exist in close proximity to each other, a large amount of socialising goes on both of nannies and of the children they are looking after. Lunches and teas are frequently had in other houses, and nannies often cook for large numbers of children. All this reduces the loneliness of a nanny spending all her time in the company of a small child. Again, this is possible because the pressure of duties is less than in the case of the mother.

As a result of this situation many children who are looked after by nannies are probably socialised more extensively at an earlier date than their peers who are cared for by their mothers. The advantage of these relationships being formed in the location of the child's home rather than, say, in a workplace nursery, is that they can be sustained at the weekends when the parents take over the caring. It is also a good way of working parents getting to know their neighbours, something which is becoming less and less common in today's society. It has the odd spin-off also of parents recognising neighbours' children in the street at weekends (from seeing them having tea with their child at home), but not having ever seen, or been introduced to, their parents. Many nannies form part of a local nanny group which may hold a weekly coffee-morning. This provides another way in which the children come into contact with others and a way for nannies to get to know one another. It is a system which is advantageous for everyone involved. The National Childbirth Trust operates nanny coffee-mornings in certain areas, advertising them in its local newsletter; others are organised on a more adhoc basis by nannies themselves.

Because the nanny only has the child and the nursery to think of, she can plan highly child-centred days and think of different ways of stimulating him. In summer, for example, lots of time can be spent outside taking picnics, weather permitting and, as they do for mothers at home, the local park and children's playground provide a meeting place. Nannies can also make use of local amenities provided initially for mothers and children, such as 1 o'clock clubs, local authority playcentres, mother and toddler groups, story-time at local libraries, and dancing lessons. Through participating in activities such as these nannies come into direct contact with mothers in the area and they can be integrated into their network. It has to be said, however, that this particular form of integration is amongst the most difficult, as at places like playgroups nannies tend to group in one corner and mothers in another. Exceptions do occur, however. This mixing is extended if a nanny is looking after a school-age child as well as a younger one, as picking up time from school is a good opportunity for people to get to know each other.

The key point in all this is that employing a nanny in

your own home means your child is not taken out of his immediate community but entrenched within it in a number of ways. Even though nannies do not stay in one employment for ever – the average time in London is probably between a year and two years, while outside London it can be a little longer – it is common for new nannies to get to know the nannies who look after established friends of their child. While personality clashes do occur, and some child friendships are suddenly halted as a result, and some new nannies may bring others into the group from a neighbouring locality if they have worked nearby previously, there remains, nonetheless, a strong core of children in the community who are kept in close contact with each other through their nannies mingling together. This pays off when school finally comes along because many of the children know each other already and this makes starting school less of a trauma.

Generally speaking the nanny can do everything with a child that a mother can do, and maybe more, simply because she has more free time at her disposal. While she is with the child she is a kind of mother substitute although she is a professional, acting at all times from experience and knowledge rather than from instinct alone. Unlike many new mothers, she knows, for example, that a screaming child can easily be distracted and will eventually stop screaming; that children are often very manipulative; and that one's demands must be consistent. Working with other children and studying childcare has given nannies a level of experience which means that they don't panic when a child falls down the stairs and know immediately what to do. It means they know that if one insists gently but firmly the child will eventually eat its vegetables. This, of course, is the ideal situation. Reality is not always so kind but there is much that is generally true in this description.

The difference in the emotional relationships between nanny and child and mother and child allows a certain distance which diminishes tensions and allows for a calm atmosphere to reign for the most part. The mother's intense fear of a child hurting itself, and anxiety about his welfare, can often create tensions which themselves cause a more emotionally loaded atmosphere than the one which exists between the nanny and the child.

If the day is largely a time of calm and stimulation coupled with quiet one-to-one moments spent reading or watching bits of children's television, the time after tea (or whenever one or the other parent arrives back home) is, in contrast, rarely so calm. Nannies must dread the moment when the child's mother walks in, back from a stressful day at work; many a well-behaved child switches into a monster, trying to punish its mother for abandoning him, implying that he has been crying from the moment she left the house, and that the nanny has mistreated him.

For the mother this is also a dreadful moment because she quickly gets to know and expect the above scenario and, although she realises that it is staged for her benefit, it still affects the blood pressure. Equally the nanny feels undermined because all the good things that have gone on in the day seem to be negated in one fell sweep. This is probably the hardest moment of the day for all three people involved and it just has to be got through with the knowledge that it is perfectly normal and that plenty of other people are going through exactly the same.

The next couple of hours, bath and bedtime, are also often difficult ones for the mother as they come at the moment of peak tiredness for everyone, when reason becomes governed by emotion and when the child has ceased to be the compliant character he was for the nanny for much of the day. For the nanny this is thankfully the moment when she can begin to drop the mantle of responsibility and switch back into her own life.

Working together

The joys of shared nurturing

Although I shall be going on to outline some of the most potentially negative aspects of a mother and a nanny working together to care for a child, it should be emphasised that there are also many benefits and pleasures to be had from this arrangement. For the mother who has some time to spend with the nanny, and is not just passing her on the threshold, there are many joys to be experienced by both people working towards the same goal together. Both parties have the best possible welfare of the child at heart and, as with many things in life, there is more pleasure to be had by sharing tasks and rewards. The humour, for instance, which most children provide during many of their waking hours is often enjoyed more when shared, likewise the intimate knowledge which both parties have of the child's idiosyncracies.

It can frequently be the case that the mother and nanny spend almost as much shared time with the child as do the mother and father. The companionship of the mother and the nanny serves to prevent the potential loneliness of both people and to reinforce and enhance the importance of stages in the child's development which can be discussed and shared. The nanny's expertise can also be an education for the mother who may have read books about child development but may not have studied the subject in any depth. Having a person, rather than a book, to consult over the emergence of a rash or a chesty cough is a privilege not to be underestimated. In many ways this relationship can take the place of the one previously formed with female relatives of the mother, when the extended family was more common and people used to live in the same street, if not in the same house, as their relatives. While it cannot replace this structure entirely – a relationship with an employee can never be exactly the same as one with a blood relative – it can come very close to it and certainly provides a similar function. Where the child is concerned, the nanny is a member of a sort of extended family, however vague that concept may be to him, and the fact that so many nannies keep in touch with children when they have ceased to take care of them, sending them birthday cards and the like, reinforces this.

Jealousy and guilt

The ideal scenario of mother, child and nanny working together in perfect harmony can be achieved, and frequently is, but it is not always easy. It may be that the personalities involved are so emotionally mature and self-reflective that not a single black cloud looms on the horizon. However, it could just as easily be the case that it is only achieved either by 'learning the hard way' or by both the mother and nanny having some painfully honest discussions together in which any frictions or tensions in the air are dissolved.

Once the practicalities of employing a nanny to help care for your child have been worked out it is then a question of learning to cope with the emotional backlash which hits most parents (especially mothers) at some time or another. Juliet Hopkins, principal child psychotherapist at the Tavistock Centre in London, has talked about the high level of anxiety that many mothers suffer when they leave their children in the care of somebody else and return to work. She describes it as 'inevitable, a throwback from our four million years as hunter gatherers. It is a protective impulse and most mothers of children under three are likely to have them in mind constantly'.

In some women this anxiety is so extreme as to force them to give up their jobs and return to the home, in others it is less severe but it is seldom entirely absent. It often takes the form of irrational fears about what is happening to the child while it is being looked after by the nanny or minder. Dr Sheila Rossan, a lecturer in psychology at Brunel University, explains, 'When I went back to work, I left my son with a retired nurse. She was a warm, competent, loving person. But I still wondered whether she was beating my child. I knew I was being irrational. But it upset me enough to make me inefficient at work.'

One explanation for such an irrational fear being directed at the child's carer is that the mother inwardly worries that in fact the child loves the carer more than he does her. This is an extremely common and understandable feeling given that the child spends so much time with the nanny and, by comparison, so little with the mother. Even the frequently-voiced arguments about the quality of time that a mother spends with her child being more important than quantity hold little sway in this context. The fundamental jealousy that a mother may feel for the nanny who looks after her child while she is at work is an emotion which most women in this situation will feel at some time or another. It is exacerbated by the confidence with which many trained nannies deal with children and can result in a sense of extreme inadequacy on the part of the mother. Typically, the nanny seldom loses her temper, she can get the child to sleep in perhaps half the time the mother takes and, with a quiet firm voice, can get a response from the child which may not be frequently forthcoming for the mother, and this does little to help things.

There is little doubt that children will do things for nannies that they will not do so readily for their parents. This is probably due to the less intense emotional tie that exists between child and nanny in most cases. This is not necessarily a comfort, however, to the mother who is in search of reassurance that her child loves her most, and sees her, and not the nanny, as the centre of his universe. These feelings are not easy ones to deal with and one cannot pretend that they do not exist nor that there is a simple solution. They are part and parcel of the three-way relationship which permits women with small children to return to work. They become dangerous and destructive, though, once they turn into resentment and this clearly must not be allowed to happen.

Jealousy can be a two-way affair, however, as the nanny can also feel that the mother intrudes upon her very close relationship with the child. It is obvious that nannies get very attached to the children they are looking after and as in any 'ménage à trois', it is natural to feel a twinge of jealousy when affection is deflected away from oneself in the direction of the third party. Once again it takes a high degree of maturity and professionalism on the part of the nanny to not find this hurtful but simply part of the job. It is also important for both mother and nanny to remember that the situation wouldn't work if the child didn't love both of them: it's simply a question of balance. Where the mother's irrational feelings are concerned she should remember that children learn very quickly and seem to accept unproblematically that nannies come and go while parents are a permanent fixture.

Another form of jealousy can come into the picture when more than one nanny has cared for a child and when both still play a part in his life. Nannies inevitably compare themselves with each other and watch to see if the child shows a greater affection for one rather than another. Human nature is highly predictable in instances like this and it is all part of the necessary protection of the child in question. What must be avoided at all costs is the formation of a competitive situation between mother and nanny or, indeed, between nannies. They must at all times remain partners in their vital job of caring as well as possible for the child in question. Any tensions will filter through to the child and create problems.

If jealousy is one aspect of the emotional backlash which can affect both mother and nanny (although probably the former to a greater degree), the related emotion, guilt, is one which attaches itself exclusively to the mother, one that has the greatest effect on her dealings both with the child and the nanny, and is, without doubt, the hardest to deal with because of its all-pervasiveness.

From the moment a mother decides to return to work after the birth of a child and to involve somebody else in the job of caring for that child, guilt enters the picture. The explanations for this universal condition are many and complex but in essence it is linked with the fact that one is abrogating a responsibility which society has expected mothers to take on for well over a century. Most of us believe that it is less a biological condition than a sociocultural one, a result of the complex conditioning process to which all women living in the western industrialised world have been subject for a considerable time. Our mothers were less likely to have done the same thing as us so we feel we are letting them down as well as our children. The reasons go on but an understanding of them does little to remove the irrational feeling that we all have about not doing for our children what we should be doing because of our need, or desire, to be part of the paid workforce.

The effects of guilt are multiple resulting either in overcompensation or resentment in the first instance. Your absence from so many of your child's waking hours may encourage you to spoil him in a number of ways – rushing out in your lunch hour, for example, to buy your child a small toy to alleviate guilt. Some mothers keep their children up when they return from work in order to spend more time with them, others feel they have to keep showering them with gifts and treats as a way of saying 'I'm sorry'. While relatively harmless, this is not an ideal situation as it means that your child comes to expect such special attention whenever you enter the picture – it clearly cannot become the norm. It may also result in the mother letting the child get away with behaviour which the nanny would consider undesirable. This has the effect of undermining the nanny's authority and in making her job considerably harder. Many working mothers fall into this trap. They feel that they spend so little time with their children that they don't want to be scolding them the entire time they are with them.

It takes a strong mother to resist this temptation but it has to be resisted at all costs. The worst possible scenario in the three-way relationship is one in which the two adults do not back up each other's decisions and actions regarding the child's behaviour. Threatened punishments (hopefully not too severe!) have to be carried through and things which have been planned or promised by one adult should not be changed by the other. In essence, the mother and nanny must as nearly as possible act as one person in the eye of the child. Where their opinions genuinely differ, this should be discussed and resolved privately. A manipulative child will be all too ready to 'divide and conquer' if the opportunity presents itself to him.

Guilt which manifests itself as resentment or nitpicking – for example, in the mother having unrealistic expectations of the nanny and feeling anger when they are not fulfilled – puts unfair pressure upon the nanny and creates a tension between the partners which will eventually make their working relationship an impossible one.

Good nannies are not insensitive to the mother's guilt. They devise strategies to deal with it and try to understand why some irrational behaviour does take place and make some allowances for it. Once again maturity is a basic requirement in this situation and with it much can be done to alleviate the effects of the destructive feelings which enter into most of our lives at some time or another.

The trouble spots

While jealousy and guilt are the most common and deep-seated emotions to rear their ugly heads in the mother-nanny-child relationship, there are a number of other areas inherent to the situation which need handling with kid gloves as they have the potential for friction. These are considerable in number and have to be confronted as they arise. However, it is worth being prepared for some of them.

The first problem which arises when a mother employs a nanny is that the child suddenly has two 'mistresses'. While a sensible mother and nanny will try to work as one authority and not undermine each other's efforts to help the child to be happy, stimulated, well-adjusted and an acceptable member of society, the child very quickly learns that it can play one adult off against the other. Thus if, for instance, nanny's demands seem to be getting a little excessive and the child really doesn't want, say, to eat his peas, he may well turn to mother and look for a reprieve. If that reprieve is forthcoming, the child has won a moral victory and will employ the same strategy again at the first possible opportunity.

This can work in reverse also. If mother has reprimanded him for something, he may well turn to the nanny for comfort. It would be a superhuman household which doesn't allow this to happen from time to time but precedents are dangerous and need to be avoided if at all possible. Once the child discovers that both adults speak with one voice he will be unable to play such effective psychological games with them in the future.

One very sensitive area for the nanny is the strong need to have sole charge of the child. Only by having the child to herself can she create a routine for him, and a set of behavioural expectations which he understands and, for the most part, to which he conforms. In order for that situation to be effective the parents should keep out of the way as much as possible when the nanny is on duty. Nothing is more irritating for a nanny than constant phone calls from the mother at work or, even worse, constant appearances at unexpected times. The mother should try to let the nanny know when she will be appearing and avoid surprises which may allow the child to attempt the 'playing one off against the other' trick. No other aspect of the nanny's job is as stressful as this one. Having the mother looking over her shoulder prevents her from doing her job properly and being able to relax in her work and employ the skills she has learnt to their full effect. Inevitably there are times when both adults are present, and indeed it is desirable that this is sometimes the case so that the child can understand that the three-way relationship exists and that it is a friction-free one. At the same time these moments should be carefully handled on the part of the mother as they are inevitably sensitive ones.

Another source of irritation to nannies is the presence of a mother who does not take part in clearing up the dishes after tea but who just expects to be waited on as, in her mind, she is telling herself that she is paying the nanny to do it. This is not the case. She is employing the nanny to help her care for her child and the notion of sharing is central to that. At the same time the nanny needs to have her tasks clearly delineated so that she knows what she is expected to do. Details like this are vital to keeping the relationship a positive one. When the mother is able to be present, she must recognise her role in the tasks at hand. While it may be fair that the mother comes home and indulges in the nice bits of childcare, like nestling up to the child near the fire with a good book, she should also be sensitive to the fact that nanny has to clear up the debris of the day. Situations such as these, as does the whole relationship, demand a respect for the other on both sides.

When mothers, or indeed fathers, work from their home thorny problems may well arise for the nanny. Coming out of the home office into the kitchen for a cup of coffee every hour is highly undesirable as it creates havoc for the nanny who has just got the child involved in a nice, calm activity such as painting or reading. The distraction caused by the intrusion of the parent is unnecessary and unforgivable and should be avoided at all costs. Office hours at home should be respected as they would be out of the house, as far as possible. The parent may choose to lunch with the child and nanny, and as long as this is part of the routine and is recognised as such by the child, then it should not present too great a problem. However, parents should expect poorer behaviour when they are present at the table than when they are absent from it. The potential for manipulation is too tempting. The nanny knows all too well that if the parent were not there she would probably be having a much quieter and more disciplined lunch.

The other problem of having a parent working at home is that the child knows that he only has to make a quick run for it and he can reach his parent and have an entertaining time poking his fingers into all sorts of interesting things which are outside his territory and therefore extremely tempting to him. He may also get an extra cuddle when nanny is reprimanding him for bad behaviour. This is a difficult one and can only be solved by repeated insistence from both parties that the office is out of bounds and that the parent will make an appearance at an appointed time and not before. Attempts by the parent to get out of the house to perform necessary tasks also have to be done by stealth as the slightest noise of the front door will suggest to the child that he has been abandoned and misery will ensue. All in all it takes an extremely long-suffering nanny to work with a child in a household in which one parent works from home.

At the other extreme, when working parents have to spend stretches of time away from home, sometimes both at the same time, the nanny who has been able to create a calm and secure routine for her child comes into her own. She is in sole charge and, providing the child knows that the parents' return is imminent (and that it will probably be accompanied by gifts) it should work without a hitch.

Parents can, of course, only do this when they have complete trust in their nanny and have established a good working relationship with her. It is a test of a strong residential nanny and hopefully will be taken in its stride. A nanny's job is never exclusively nine to five, however, or even seven to seven, as some baby-sitting is part of the agreement and it may well be the case that parents go out for the evening directly from work and the nanny will be expected to perform all the bath and bedtime rituals. It is often more desirable for this pattern to occur as once parents return home it can be difficult for them to get out of the house again without dramatic scenes.

Parents working at home may not be the only people who get in the way of a nanny performing her tasks, however. Visiting grandparents and aunts and uncles, can also be a burden if they don't respond to the situation sensitively. While a nanny is able to vet parents at the job interview she cannot do the same with their relations and she may find that she has to spend time with adoring grandparents whose views of how you bring up a child differ considerably from her own. This is a very trying situation which has to be dealt with carefully as grandparents are unlikely to be familiar with the concept of the modern nanny, may even disapprove of their daughter or daughter-in-law working, and are probably watchful as to how their beloved grandchild is being looked after. Grandparents who live nearby, or even on the premises, need to be told by the parents that the nanny is in charge of things and that this needs to be respected for their sake. To look on the positive side, grandparents can be extra company, an extra pair of hands and the reason for an excursion if they live nearby.

The other potentially problematic areas involved in employing a nanny concern the degree to which the parents and the nanny resolve differences of opinion as to how the child is to be looked after and brought up. This is at the very heart of the parent-nanny-child relationship and key areas include the questions of what the child should be given to eat, whether he should be given sweets, how much television or video he should watch, how much time he should spend at the shops or in other people's houses, and whether he should be reprimanded about his manners or lack of them. In all these areas the parents have instinctive feelings, based most probably on the ways in which they were brought up themselves, about what should or shouldn't happen (they may disagree between themselves which intensifies the problem). The nanny also has her ideas, acquired either through books or experience. Sometimes these ideas are happily in line with each other and sometimes not. One has to remember that approaches to childcare move in generational waves like any other and that parents and nannies are unlikely to be members of the same generation.

When there is disagreement the only thing to do is to discuss it and hope to reach a compromise. If the differences are too great (and that should have been ironed out at the interview stage) then you probably have to agree to part company. If there are small differences, however – mother wants no sweets, for example, but nanny thinks a couple after tea are harmless and will prevent the child building up a craving for them in later years – then a compromise can probably be reached. The mother should acknowledge to herself that in employing a nanny one cannot impose **all** one's beliefs on the way in which her child is brought up. At the same time a mother might be adamant, for example, that she doesn't want her children getting down from the table before they ask to do so and the nanny might be a little lax about this. In this case, after discussion, it would not seem unreasonable to ask the nanny to be a little firmer if only to please the mother. The question of manners is an area which people develop opinions about largely on the basis of their own childhood (whether emulating it or opposing it) and, of course, there is also a class component. Middle-class table manners are not absolutes but rather a shared code and if a mother wants her child to adhere to it then it is up to her to ask the nanny to act accordingly.

Diet is a more complex question as it relates to health and not just to social mores. Most nannies know about nutrition from their training but some mothers have strong views about their children not eating certain things or, for example, keeping their food entirely free from artificial additives. The problem can be solved for the most part by the parents doing the shopping and thereby determining what is in stock, but they cannot legislate entirely for the odd packet of crisps full of E numbers which creeps into the house through the back door. Again moderation and discussion are called for here. While mother's wishes must be respected as far as possible, it is the nanny who prepares most of the child's meals and she cannot be expected to make everything from fresh, additive-free ingredients if all the child really wants, and more to the point will actually eat, is beans on toast or fishfingers. Naturally, it is important to combine realism with idealism in a case such as this.

The diet issue arises especially when, as is the case with children being cared for by nannies, a lot of meals are taken in other people's houses. Here it is often a question of eating what you are served. Much has to be left to the discretion of the nanny in this instance as she cannot ring up the mother on every visit out to ask whether the child in question is allowed to have beefburgers!

As with manners, the views on how much television is good for a child are socially determined to a large extent.

Many middle-class mothers would rather that their children saw as little as possible as they feel it encourages passivity and makes children immune to some of the stronger emotions. But nannies have to find a way of creating space in the day when food can be prepared or ironing done and neither of these tasks can be performed with a child holding on to your legs. Some children sleep very little through the day but need a rest period where there is a minimum of stimulation around them. There are enough good childrens' television programmes on the air to fill these moments and it is very common for nannies to use television for these specific ends. Once again ideals hit pragmatics in the day-to-day world of childcare. The mother, removed from the details of the daily routine, is in a good position to think about the ideals underpinning child development. The nanny is more locked into strategies involved in getting through the day in as effective a way as possible. Once again the two views need to be discussed and a middle path found where appropriate.

Perhaps the most emotive of all the potential areas of friction between a child's parents and its nanny is the question of discipline. Once again this is frequently dominated by the mother's guilt which results in her not wanting to punish the child but rather to grant it favours as a means of alleviating her own guilt feelings. Nannies usually have a more straightforward approach to discipline which involves carrying through threats as a means of remaining credible in the eyes of the child. Thus a nanny who says 'If you don't finish your carrots you can't have any pudding' means it and will carry out what she promises. Working mothers often find it harder to go through with such threats and become the soft option to the child. Clearly this is an untenable situation as it immediately offers the child scope for manipulation. Because the nanny spends so much time with the child she must have an ultimate deterrent which allows her to retain a level of control. Whether it is 'Go to your room and don't come out until I tell you you can', or 'Sit on the bottom of the stairs until we have finished our tea', these punishments have to be implemented if the nanny is to perform her role effectively. It may be difficult for the mother, coming in from work and wanting a hug, to back the nanny up when she sees her tearful child hugging the bannister, but that is exactly what she has to do if she wants to keep an equilibrium in the household and keep the three-way relationship in harmony.

The question of what punishment is suitable must, of course, have been previously discussed by the parents and the nanny together. If parents want a child smacked then they must say so and the nanny must say how she feels about that. If smacking is to be avoided at all costs then the nanny must respect that also. Above all the child cannot be allowed to think that he has the upper hand where discipline is concerned because he knows that his parents and his nanny disagree about what kind of punishment is appropriate. It is a golden rule, also, that parents must back a nanny's action in front of the child (within reason, of course) even if they disagree with it and take it up with her later.

The other key area of debate between parents and the nanny concerning the child's welfare has to do with development. The best way to encourage walking, talking, for instance, and to potty-train a child, are all matters which need to be discussed. When and how, for example, are they to be done? In these areas there can be a high level of nanny leading and mother following as the former probably has more experience than the latter. At the same time, the parents want to feel involved and they probably have their own ideas about how they would like things done. The nanny has, therefore, to be careful to allow them a role in things. As in many other of the aspects of childcare, part of the nanny's job is, in fact, to make the parents think that they are involved and playing a key part even in things which go on when they are at their workplaces.

The last area of possible friction that I shall mention here doesn't involve the child and its welfare but has more bearing on the way the parents and nanny interrelate as co-habitants. A family consisting of father, mother and small child may find it difficult to allow another adult to enter into its domestic space and become part of the household. It may find it difficult to have someone else eating in its kitchen, using its telephone, driving its car and generally invading what has hitherto been its private territory. One has even heard extreme cases of the wife becoming jealous because the husband was paying too much attention to the young girl who was suddenly in their midst. Problems like these are beyond the scope of this book but they demonstrate the manner in which a new element in the household can sometimes cause friction and resentment. It might be that the nanny eats the piece of cake that you had deliberately left as a treat for yourself; it may be that your privacy is rudely interrupted when you are entertaining friends. The possible scenarios are endless.

What must be remembered is that this is all part of what having the security and convenience of a live-in nanny is all about. It is important to recognise the positive aspects of that decision and to minimise what may at first seem like the negative ones as with time, they will disappear as a problem. As the nanny becomes involved in the household she becomes an integral part of it very easily. Part of her professionalism is not to intrude but to glide invisibly into the household while becoming an essential element within it. It is also vital to remember that the parents are in the position of power as they outnumber the nanny and own the house. As a result they must be extra sensitive to the need for the nanny to feel at home – this is her home from now on after all – and to make her feel welcome and part of things, to the extent to which she wishes to be so.

One could go on with the list of situations and areas which, if not addressed sensibly and with maturity, could give rise to problems when one employs a live-in nanny. In the end both disasters and huge successes occur for as many different reasons as why people do and don't get on with each other and do and don't act stupidly. There is no sure formula for success but it helps to reflect on the full ramifications of the situation into which one is entering when one employs a live-in nanny and to decide that you are going to do everything within your power to make a success of it for the sake, in the last analysis, of the child whose welfare this is all about.

Beyond routine

While the day-to-day relationship between parents and nannies can be an extremely fruitful one, and highly beneficial to the child in question, it is nonetheless, like any other form of human relationship, dependent upon a great deal of sustained effort from all parties involved. Just when one feels that one has overcome the majority of the potential hazards of the situation and established a workable routine which is acceptable to everyone involved, a non-routine occurrence comes along and upsets the apple cart.

Illness

The illness of any of the people involved in the parent-nanny-child relationship can cause problems all round. If the child is ill the parents' natural anxieties are heightened and the calm which had been established goes into reverse. At the same time it is an advantage to have another pair of hands around in emergency situations, especially a pair which are used to children's illnesses and accidents and able to cope with them in a professional manner. While every parent hopes that they will have the common sense to throw their child under the cold water tap if they scald themselves, there is the danger that panic and shock will delay things. Nannies usually act quickly in these circumstances and are a definite asset to have around.

A mother's illness is problematic inasmuch as once the child knows that she is in the house, she is unlikely to get much peace and the nanny's job is made increasingly difficult as a result. Even more serious, from the point of view of the smooth running of things, is the nanny's illness. If she is out of action, the system, delicate at the best of times, can break down completely. It is one thing for a parent to take time off work if they are ill themselves, it is another to persuade an employer that mother needs to stay at home because the nanny is ill. As a result it becomes a very difficult problem to circumvent and nannies tend to work until they drop, knowing that if they give up problems will ensue.

The various solutions to this particular problem include hauling in a member of the family, a neighbour or, as quite commonly happens, a nearby nanny. Many nannies provide a back-up system for each other in these circumstances knowing that it will benefit everyone in the long run. Providing that the employer is making the proper national insurance payments, sick pay is available so nobody loses out financially. These times are considered by all concerned to be inconveniences which have to be got over one way or another and a number of adhoc solutions usually appear to make sure that they pass as smoothly as possible.

If it proves impossible to find somebody to help out who is familiar to the child in question – clearly the most desirable solution – the last resort is to employ a temporary nanny from the agencies which offer such a service. Most of the agencies which can provide a full-time nanny also offer a temporary nanny service on a daily or weekly basis.

While this may seem like a desperate move, it can in fact work very well as the nannies who work in this way are highly professional and experts in handling a child who is not familiar with them. Indeed the child often sees it as a novelty, having someone new to come and read books to him, feed him and change his nappies. As with many other circumstances which arise when employing a nanny, any problem can be overcome providing a child knows that its parents are permanent fixtures and that nannies are, to a certain extent, moveable feasts.

Holidays

The main question which arises when you are planning your annual holiday is whether the nanny will come with you or not. A nanny is entitled to around four weeks paid holiday a year. If she comes on holiday with you this is considered work and she will need to make up her holiday at another time. Given the likely holiday allowance of the parents this might cause difficulties as it will mean that they are without a nanny for a couple of weeks or so. Ways round this include offering to pay your nanny extra to work through her holidays (some are saving up and would appreciate this opportunity); taking on a temporary nanny for a couple of weeks; or falling back again on family and friends.

Many parents, however, don't want their nannies to accompany them on holiday simply because this is a unique opportunity for some quality time alone with their children. Most parents who employ nannies don't do so because they want their children out of their sight as much as possible but because work is important to them for various reasons and so a compromise has to be reached.

Any opportunity to spend time with the children outside working hours is, therefore, dedicated to the children and enjoyed to the full. If this is the case then it is important to give the nanny plenty of warning as to when you intend to take your holiday if you expect her to plan hers at the same time. She probably has friends to liaise with and bookings to make and this can take some time to organise.

It may turn out, however, that one parent has a longer vacation than the other and wants to go away somewhere hot alone with the children and would like to take the nanny along both as a pair of extra hands and as company. Or indeed there may be so many small children in a family that parents can't imagine getting anything out of a holiday at all if they don't take some help along. It may also simply be that you're going somewhere exotic and it's an opportunity of showing your gratitude to the nanny by taking her along for the holiday of a lifetime. In all these circumstances the question of how the group dynamic will work when you are all away together needs to be thought through as the situation will be dramatically different from that of the normal routine at home.

The nanny will be more dependent upon you for company on holiday as her network of friends will not be around, and you will almost certainly all want to eat together in the evenings and go on trips out together. Suddenly you are all more like a single unit than before and everyone will muck in as best they can. Two things are important to remember in this situation. The first is that the child will need to be able to understand why you are all suddenly together and how your roles in relation to him will function. Secondly, while this is a working holiday for the nanny, it is still a form of holiday and just because she is now around all day and night and not disappearing at six o'clock, she should not be made to feel as if she is on duty all the time. Sunbathing can be done in rotas as can the preparation of meals and the washing of clothes. Holidays with nannies and children are an ideal opportunity for you all to get to know each other much better and for a good time to be had by all.

Special occasions

One of the most enjoyable, if exhausting, aspects of having a small child is preparing for feasts and celebrations such as birthdays and Christmas. Once again the parent should be willing to share that fun with the nanny as she needs high spots to break with the routine as much as, if not more than, the parents do. Many nannies plunge into the preparation of a child's party with enormous enthusiasm and are much better able and have more time than the mother to make and decorate a novelty cake, put together a fancy dress costume, and organise a set of imaginative children's games. She probably also knows, much better than the mother, which children to invite and what presents would go down best.

This is another time when mother and nanny need to work together closely, planning a menu, shopping for food and preparing it. Nannies may also be much better than the mother at being the 'master of ceremonies' at the event itself and, even if it is held on a weekend day, would wish to perform this role. (An extra day's pay does not go amiss in these circumstances.)

One approach to the question of the child's birthday is actually to hold two events, one on a week day organised and attended by local nannies and the children they look after – probably the child's closest companions – and the other at the weekend for the parents' friends, family and attached children who form the child's other peer group. These two groups tend to have distinct identities and are probably best kept separate. This will change significantly when a child starts school and picks his own friends from amongst his schoolmates.

A new baby

One of the most difficult things for any child to accept is the arrival of a new baby in the household. When there is a live-in nanny around, and the mother is at home on maternity leave with a new baby, the interrelationship of the people involved needs to be thought through carefully. Inevitably much of the mother's time will be spent with the new baby but she will want to involve the older child as much as possible so that he doesn't feel left out or rejected. While the mother may need the nanny's help with the baby to a certain extent, the child will probably feel that the nanny is there exclusively for him and indeed she can play an important role helping him adapt to the new situation by being there 'especially' for him. Thus, for example, while the mother is feeding the baby the nanny can do something intimate with the child, such as reading him a story. While the mother is taking a rest in the afternoon the nanny can take the child out to the library and choose books especially for him. In this way he feels that he is not being neglected, that some time is being carved out for him, and this makes his acceptance of the new baby easier than it might otherwise have been.

When the mother returns to work after her maternity leave, however, the situation changes quite dramatically as suddenly the nanny has to spend time comforting a screaming baby and changing nappies, as well as looking after the existing child. It is at this point that the nanny has to employ careful strategies to ensure that a balance is maintained and the parents need to back up those strategies to make things work. In some ways having a nanny around in these circumstances makes things easier all round but it involves a degree of planning so that all the people involved are working in unison with each other.

Caring for more than one child is always a more complicated operation than looking after one on its own although the compensations include the children playing with each other once they are old enough to do so. With two or more children in her care, a nanny needs to develop a fairly strict routine to ensure that things work smoothly. With an expanded family to look after, a nanny's salary should go up to reflect the extra work involved.

Starting school

The moment when a child starts full-time school is the point at which parents have to think again about their childcare arrangements as there is little point having a trained, well-paid childcarer back at home twiddling her thumbs waiting for the school day to end. There are arguments for keeping a nanny on a half-day basis when children attend school as that gives time for all the chores to be done during the child's absence thereby giving them full-time attention once they are home. Beyond that, however, it doesn't make economic or common sense to carry on.

The situation is, however, a very different one if a nanny looks after a number of siblings, at least one of which is of pre-school age. It can even work out to be the most economic option when three or more children are concerned. In circumstances such as these a nanny may well be around when one of the children starts school and have to cope with all the implications of that change in routine. For one thing it means that, if the nanny is taking the child to school and picking him up, which is very likely, the routine of the day is dictated by those activities and the other children have to fit in with it. At the school gates the nanny will either mix with other nannies who are doing the same thing, or with parents who are picking up their children. Here the two 'cultures' – mother-culture and nanny-culture – mix relatively openly, and this is encouraged by the child asking to have classmates back to tea. Looking after a schoolchild helps a nanny become part of the larger community, therefore, and requests for babysitting from other mothers are often in abundance. In essence the nanny plays the role that a mother would when looking after a schoolchild, making sure that messages get back, keeping the lines of communication open between the parents and the school, ensuring that the child has a chance to talk about all the things he did during the day, and admiring all the pictures he brings home.

At this point also the schoolchild tends to assume that the nanny is there essentially for his younger siblings and that he has a direct link with his parents who also go out to work all day. Suddenly he has more in common with them than with those who have been left at home and the balance within the relationships shifts accordingly. The advantages of having a full-time nanny in the home when you have one or more schoolchildren become obvious when half-term, school holidays and illnesses come along.

Changing nannies

Although some nannies stay with a pre-school child from

early days through to school this is fairly unusual, and you can generally count on a nanny staying with you for between one and two years (probably longer outside London). On average a pre-school child may have between two and five nannies looking after him. Any more than this is undesirable and you would either be unlucky or a bad employer if that occurred.

Because so many nannies are professionals they have a career structure in front of them. They need, in order to advance their careers, to have a broad spectrum of experiences, including looking after a range of children from babyhood to school age; living out and living in; working in the provinces, London and abroad. At the same time they need a good set of references so they must stay in each position long enough to do an effective job before they think of moving on to the next experience. Another reason for moving on is because they get very attached to the children they are looking after and they have often to break ties in order to protect themselves from too much pain. In many ways it is a good thing for all concerned that the relationship doesn't get so intense that a break becomes very difficult. It is a problem for the mother if the nanny has become so attached to the children that she doesn't want to leave them inasmuch as it jeopardises the former's position and creates an unhealthy situation all round. There is also a natural period of time during which enthusiasm pulls everything along and then the repetitiveness of routine begins to dull the edges of that enthusiasm.

Whatever the reasons for a family and a nanny deciding to part company, and there could be many of them (it may be that the family want to start thinking about a new arrangement as their children start school, or it may be that the nanny feels it is time to move on), whichever party came to that decision owes it to the other to give the longest possible period of notice. While contractually they are only obliged to give a month, it is desirable if the discussion about change could come well before that as both sides want to be able to plan their next move in good time. It might be that a mother asks the nanny if she could postpone her plans until the summer or the nanny might just want to warn the parents that she planned to give her notice in at Christmas.

If the nanny is moving on to another, albeit different, kind of nanny post and the parents intend to employ another nanny, then both sides can begin to take some action, namely, register with agencies, buy a copy of *The Lady*, put out feelers locally, and generally help each other in their respective searches.

When the time comes for the new nanny to start it can be a good idea to have a day, or at most two, of overlap not simply so that one can show the other how to use the dishwasher and the microwave but also so that she can introduce her to the local network, something which the mother is not in such a good position to do. The outgoing nanny can also pass on tips as to how to handle the child and, indeed, the parents. These few days can save weeks of a new nanny finding her feet in the cold. If the two nannies don't hit it off, which is possible but unprofessional, then it is not so long that any damage will have been done. The mother (or indeed father) should also ideally spend some time with the new nanny, showing her the ropes but also explaining her preferences and the way things have worked best in the past. There is a danger, however, of intimidating a new nanny by overemphasising the success of her predecessor so it is possibly best to underplay this.

The most important thing when a nanny changeover occurs is that the minimum of disruption occurs and that the child feels that the change is a seamless one. This may mean that the new nanny has to modify her thoughts a little about the way she would ideally like to do things in order to sustain continuity – if a child had a sleep in the early afternoon, for example, this should be continued for a while even if the new nanny thinks this is utterly wrong. The child must come first and everything must be decided upon in his best interests.

A smooth changeover is desirable for all concerned – for the child, for the new nanny, for the outgoing nanny who then feels that she can maintain contact with the child and with the family, and, above all, for the parents who can once more relax a little as they face the next stage in the ever-changing scenario of bringing up children alongside working full-time.

Other options

The scenario of the live-in nanny caring for one or more children belonging to a single family is only one among other options available to the working mother. The live-out, or daily, nanny has already been mentioned but there are also other, cheaper ways of going about obtaining this kind of childcare. Many people share nannies, either live-out or live-in, while a lower paid alternative (although not for mothers working on a full-time basis) could be to employ somebody who is described as a 'mother's help' rather than a nanny.

The live-out nanny

If you haven't got room to have a nanny living on the premises with you, or if you cannot bear the idea of sharing your space with someone outside your immediate family unit for 24 hours a day, then a live-out nanny may well be the most appropriate form of childcare for you. Because a nanny in this situation has to pay for her own accommodation and most of her living expenses, she will command a significantly higher salary, however. This makes it a prohibitive option for many people and it is, as a result, relatively uncommon, except, that is, where a share is involved.

The advantages of having a nanny come to your house on a daily basis include the fact that she is likely to be settled in your locality – she may even be married – and may therefore stay with you for longer than a nanny who lives 'on the job'. Dailies are best contacted through local sources, whether through the local further education college if you want somebody who has just finished their training, or through the local paper or newsagent's window.

Daily nannies want to get back to their own homes in the evening and, although they may be prepared to do some babysitting for extra pocket money, they naturally enough prefer to get away at the time their contract states that they should. Arriving home later than predicted should always be avoided, but fighting your way back through rush-hour traffic makes it unavoidable at times. In this situation a live-in nanny who is not thinking about her journey home through the traffic as well offers a little more flexibility. Dailies are sometimes less inclined to stay and tell you about everything that happened in the day and so keeping the lines of communication open can be a little harder in these circumstances. Some people are happy to put up with this, though, for what they consider to be the delight of having their home to themselves in the evenings and weekends.

Sharing a nanny

Because nannies are expensive, but have the advantage in many people's eyes of being able to look after a child in its own home, arranging to share one with another family seems a sensible alternative. It is also worth taking into account that childminders, the obvious alternative to the nanny, are paid per child and that once two children are involved it may well cost less to share a nanny rather than pay a childminder for both children. The economics of childcare become more complicated when two or more children are involved and balancing out the pros and cons of one system as opposed to another, and working out the best option where both economics and the most desirable situation for the children are concerned, takes some thought.

While nanny-sharing is clearly an attractive proposition, it also needs careful thought as the possible scenarios to be encountered can be very complex. The first difficulty is how to find the right nanny-share for you. This is clearly more tricky than taking on a nanny as her sole employer, where agencies and the national press play a useful role. Involving yourself in a nanny-share is, of course, dependent upon finding another family, located near enough to make it feasible, which has either the same or complementary requirements of a nanny. The best way to find out whether or not such a family exists is to contact a local nanny-share register – branches of both the National Childbirth Trust and the Working Mothers Association should be able to help in this context – or to spread the word locally, through whatever means, that you are on the look-out for a share of this kind. Health Centres, newsagents' windows, local libraries and schools are all good places in which to make it known that you are looking for a nanny-share. Even putting notes through peoples' doors is a possibility if things get desperate. For the most part agencies find this sort of thing a little too complicated and not financially viable enough for them. Clearly you need to start looking around as soon as possible as it can take time to first match yourself up with someone and then to find the right nanny for both of you.

Another strategy is to take on a nanny as her sole employer for a short period until you find someone who can share her with you (providing of course that she is keen to do this). There are financial risks in this course of action, but it means that you have something to offer your potential partner. Equally you may find a family which already has a nanny and which would like to share her with you.

Whichever course of action you take to find a share it is important to be absolutely sure that the situation is a totally workable one, and to go through all the possible permutations, combinations and eventualities with your fellow employer and the nanny before any commitments are made. The most common nanny-share consists of two pre-school children of a similar age. This provides few problems for a trained nanny: it is no more demanding, in fact, than having twins or two siblings to care for. The real difficulty comes, however, when there is less than a year between two very young children who are being looked after by one nanny as their sleeping and eating timetables can get very complex. It is important, therefore, in this situation to ensure that things like the diet, sleep times and general routines of both children are compatible. The extra expense incurred by this arrangement might well be the joint purchase of a double buggy, or of other pieces of equipment, such as an additional cot, which make it possible for the nanny to care for both children at the same time in the same house.

Another common share arrangement is for a nanny who has only school age children, whom she picks up from school, to take on a pre-school child from another family to fill up her time during the day. This requires a lot of sensitivity if it is to be handled successfully as the school children must not be made to feel that they are playing second fiddle to this younger child. They can, however, play a large part in helping care for it as well, if the situation is handled carefully.

The question of whether the shared nanny is a daily or whether she lives in the house of one of her employers needs resolving, as does the location in which the children are to be looked after. Frequently nannies will occupy one house for one week and the other house for the next, or if they live very near, one for one day and one for the next. This means that both families are involved equally in covering all the expenses incurred, and in suffering wear and tear to their houses. Sometimes only one house is used and the other family will contribute to the upkeep of the premises and the expenses. Who is going to do the paperwork involved with the nanny's tax and insurance payments also needs to be resolved at the outset.

The most important thing, however, is for you to be sure that your employer–partner shares your ideas about the ways in which the children are to be cared for. Not only is it the nanny with whom you must discuss things like television, sweets, and shopping. You must also see eye to eye with the sharer or conflicting messages could be in the air and the poor nanny won't know what to do for the best. The nanny also needs to employ extreme tact in a nanny-share as she cannot enter into the dangerous activity of discussing one employer with the other behind her back. Communication – three ways in this case – is more vital than ever in a nanny-share if all parties are to feel happy with the situation.

The plus side of a nanny-share includes two families and their children getting to know each other well and becoming very close; less expense for both families but a higher salary for the nanny than if she had a single employer (plus very good Christmas and birthday presents!); and having a strong back-up system on the doorstep when illness and other emergencies strike. The minus side includes dealing constantly with a complicated set of arrangements – what time does the baby need to be delivered and picked up? Which house are we in this week? When can we all take our holidays so that it suits everyone including the nanny's boyfriend? It also includes losing a degree of individual attention for the children involved and having to remain extremely flexible and tolerant throughout the whole arrangement.

Nanny-shares are also less able to adapt to the arrival of a new baby which would probably put excessive strain upon an already tight arrangement. The nanny and her employers have to think very carefully about the next move when another pregnancy occurs on either side. Does she become the sole employee of one family? Does she leave completely? Could more help be brought in from somewhere else? The nanny is quite vulnerable in this situation as she is more likely, than in a non-share situation, to have to rethink her role completely. It demands a great deal of maturity and can only be undertaken by a highly experienced nanny who knows what is, and what is not, possible. The maximum number of pre-school children a nanny can cope with must be three (the number the law permits a childminder to look after) and that can push things to the limit if the children's diets, ages, routines and temperaments are not compatible with each other. If more than one of the children is under the age of two then dealing with a third child could be very difficult unless he is at school for most of the day. Overburdening a nanny means that she is turned into a minder rather than a carer and this is not what most nannies have been trained for and, therefore, not the job they want to do.

If a nanny works for more than two employers (a fairly

rare situation) she must, like all childminders, be registered with the local authority. Many people would like that law extended and to see the introduction of a local register for all nannies. This, they feel, would go some way towards keeping a check upon all childcare in the home and to giving mothers greater peace of mind when leaving their children with carers for long stretches of time. While the serious problems that have occurred with trained or experienced nannies in the home seem to be very few in number and the standard of caring is for the most part extremely high, there is always an element of risk in this area as parents are left entirely on their own to make decisions about who to employ to look after their children.

Nanny-shares need to be approached in such a way to ensure that the nanny appointed is not being exploited and that quality care is maintained. The temptation to save money in this situation must, of course, be offset by the need for each child in question to receive the highest possible standard of care. This ensured, sharing a nanny can be a very rewarding and enjoyable experience for everybody involved.

The mother's help

Perhaps even more than the shared nanny the mother's help is open to a high degree of exploitation which must be avoided at all costs. There have been instances when families have advertised for, and employed, a mother's help rather than a nanny because it was cheaper, and because somebody answering this job description is prepared to do general housework and help with the weekly shopping as well as look after the children. This misconception must be completely abandoned, however, as a mother's help could be somebody who wants to work in a domestic situation with young children but who has no training in this field so far, and possibly little direct experience. It could, on the other hand, be somebody who was the eldest child in a large family and who is more than capable of looking after small children and a house single-handed. Whichever mother's help is in question it must be stressed that the role of somebody with this title is to assist the mother in the home, both with light household tasks and with childcare, but who is not to be left in a sole charge situation. They can be employed either on a live-in or on a daily basis; many might want to go on to be nannies later, but are for the time being simply in the business of getting some experience. Inevitably mothers' helps are paid less than nannies – at the time of writing, somewhere between £50 and £80 a week if they are residential.

A large number of girls from abroad travelling in England – especially from Australia and New Zealand – use the opportunity of working as a mother's help as a means of living with a British family, learning more about British life and earning some money. This is an ideal arrangement for all concerned but not necessarily very long-lived as these girls have all been bitten with the travel bug and are preparing to move on to their next European port of call or to go back home. Other mothers' helps are older, local women, maybe with school-aged or grown-up children of their own. Yet others can be very young British school-leavers who have not really decided what they want to do in life and are just killing a bit of time before they commit themselves to anything on a more permanent basis.

At most, a mother's help might help you out if you work on a part-time basis or if you work from home in a flexible manner. They are in no circumstances the adequate child-care answer for a full-time working mother.

PART 3

Caring outside the home

Opting for a childminder

Childminding is the most popular form of paid childcare in Great Britain today. Nineteen per cent of all estimated children in childcare are looked after by childminders and it is thought that there are at present over 80,000 childminders looking after around 300,000 children. This number has risen sharply over the last decade.

While this is largely a result of the fact that nursery provision, especially for children under the age of two, is so inadequate, and that employing a nanny (with the exception of a nanny-share in certain circumstances) is, for the most part, more expensive, there are undoubtedly a number of other reasons why people may decide that they don't want a nanny but that they would rather take their children to be looked after by somebody who will care for them in her own home.

For many people the idea of a young, trained nanny is less desirable as an adequate mother substitute for their child than the 'real thing', which, for them, is somebody who has her own children and has learnt to look after them through trial and error. This, for them, is somebody who understands what maternal feelings are all about and for whom childcare has become a way of life rather than a career. Others also find it easier to take their child somewhere out of the home and therefore not have to bother about providing toys, food, and all the rest of the paraphernalia that are essential parts of his daily routine. For some it is simply an economic matter: they can't afford a nanny and are happy to opt for the cheaper solution, a childminder. Alternatively, they can see the benefits that undoubtedly derive from their child becoming part of the local community, a spin-off which can come from using a childminder who, unlike a live-in nanny, is already part of it herself. Lastly for some the idea of employing someone in their own home is simply anathema, a middle-class activity which is utterly alien to their way of life.

Whatever the reasons for opting for a childminder, there's a complex culture which surrounds the world of childminding which needs to be confronted and understood. The best way of learning about it is to experience it at first hand but this chapter is intended to act as a broad introduction to some of its chief characteristics.

It is important to remember that the childminding system is one in which the state, through the channel of the social services department of the local authority, has a part to play. All childminders have to be registered with their local authority if they are looking after children under the age of eight. The state takes an active role in checking that minders' premises are safe enough for young children. They also do some research on the individual childminder in question, looking into their medical history and checking to see whether or not they have a police record. In addition there are rules controlling what a childminder can and cannot do. She cannot, for example, look after more than three pre-school age children, including her own, and only one of these can be under a year old. This involvement on the part of the local authority is a very positive aspect of using a childminder as nannies are not monitored in the same way. It does not, however, include looking at the standards of the childcare in question. That is left for the parents to assess.

The National Childminding Association, founded in 1977, has done a lot of work helping to raise standards and to improve the image of the childminder, which is still a Dickensian one in many ways. Today minders are used by a cross section of society and provide a useful and necessary service in an age when so many women want to go back to work after the birth of their children. It is, however, an option which, compared to employing a nanny, can include a certain loss of control. For this reason it is vital that the implications of using a childminder are fully considered before you enter into this particular option, but there is no reason why, if this is done, it cannot be a fully satisfactory arrangement.

At home or not?

A fundamental question that has to be asked when choosing between a nanny or a childminder to look after your child is whether you think that he is better off, or not, being cared for in his own home. This is really an emotional matter rather than one which has definite psychological or developmental implications, and there is no final consensus about which is the right, and which is the wrong, answer to the question.

While some parents feel strongly that a young child is best looked after in his own home, others will feel equally strongly that putting him into another home does no harm, and that, in fact, it provides an extra level of important stimulus for a child to get to know another domestic environment as well as he does his own. It is argued that much time is already spent at home – mornings, evenings, nights and weekends – and that familiarity with someone else's home (providing, of course, that it is a secure and happy one) can only enrich the child's life. Those who advocate the 'in his own home' approach are more influenced by the idea of security than that of stimulus. They feel that just one familiar setting is necessary as a secure base within which the child can develop to his full potential, both physically and mentally.

There is no proof that either side is entirely correct or wrong and, of course, different solutions are right for different parents and different children. Parents' feelings mostly come from the 'gut' in this area and cannot be rationalised completely. If history has anything to offer to this debate it is the fact, perhaps, that the concept of the 'home' as a necessary psychological, as well as physical, environment, is a relatively new invention dating back at most 200 years. It came into being at the same time as 'the separation of the spheres', that is, when men moved into the factories to work and women stayed at home to rear children and manage the upkeep of the household. With this came what has been called the Cult of Domesticity which has probably had a lot to do with our feelings in the present day that there is something special about a child's own home as the most important site for his development.

As in so many other areas linked with motherhood and children our cultural conditioning has a lot to answer for. The discussion can go on and on without, of course, there being an answer to it. It's a matter, in the end, for individuals to make up their own minds about what they feel is best for their child and to act accordingly.

Who costs less?

The key practical question influencing the choice of a nanny or a childminder, however, is their comparative costs. In the last section I outlined the approximate cost of employing a nanny as a sole employer. It can be a significant undertaking. If one takes the average salary of a nanny to be, at the time of writing, around £120 a week, and adds the tax and insurance payments which would be around £40 a week, and, in addition, the live-in expenses which probably average out to at least £20 a week, one reaches the weekly total of about £180. This would be a little more if more than one child was involved. (It could be halved, of course, if a nanny-share was entered into.) By comparison the recommended rate of each child to be looked after by a childminder is, at the time of writing, around £1.10 an hour (rising to around £2 in some parts of London). The average payment for a childminder is, therefore, around £45 a week, but it could be a little more. If two children are involved then it is easy to see how close the cost is between using a childminder or a nanny-share to look after your children. Of course, many other variables enter the situation and the choice to be made, however, among them the ages and natures of the children in question. What is certain is that if a single baby is involved, a childminder is a considerably cheaper option than a nanny employed as his sole carer.

With only one child, also, the money you pay a childminder is not enough to be taxed and you are therefore spared the work involved with making payments to the tax man. In addition, because most minders are paid by the hour, or the day, different arrangements come into being during holidays and times of illness. Many different possibilities exist here but usually only a percentage of the cost is payable at certain times, and at others none at all. Some minders, for example, expect something from you during your holidays but nothing during theirs. Conditions vary from situation to situation, but, generally speaking, some savings can be made when using a childminder. In contrast the nanny is paid on a yearly salary basis. Equally, however, nannies wouldn't usually charge overtime if you are home a little late one evening whereas a minder would be well within her rights to do so. Lastly, your payment to the minder includes the cost of the child's meals as agreed between you, domestic overheads such as heating and electricity and any toys and equipment that are used during the course of the day.

Who's the best person?

If money is no obstacle, and you are open-minded about whether you want your child to be looked after in his own home or not, there are still some other things to take into consideration when weighing up whether to opt for a nanny or a childminder. You should, for example, think through the question of what sort of person you would feel confident about looking after your child. Would you like somebody who has studied childcare theory and who knows what to do during the various developmental stages because she has learnt all about them and probably tested out her knowledge through experience? Or would you prefer somebody who has had her own children and knows what to do but who has learnt the hard way by following her instincts and seeing what works best through trial and error? The knowledge of the latter has been built up in a more adhoc manner but there is no reason to assume that it is any less sound. Indeed, for many mothers, the common-sense approach can be much more appealing because it is grounded in practical rather than abstract theory. Many first-time mothers, in fact, find the childminder a source of common-sense advice and confidence-building. For some indeed she can perform the role of a mother substitute, introducing them to the mysterious world of motherhood, in a way a young girl straight off the NNEB course never could. Age is a consideration in this discussion as nannies are mostly in their twenties whereas childminders are usually older, either having reared, or still in the process of rearing, a family of their own.

Another question you should consider is the motivation behind both the nanny and the minder to want to look after your child. The nanny has most probably opted for a career with young children as opposed to one, say, in an office, bank or other similar environment. She is highly committed, therefore, to taking an active role in relation to the child she is looking after as this is the essence of the way in which she defines her job. Minders, on the other hand, often come to their task in a different way. For them, kept at home with a family, it is one of the few options available to them to earn some money and the one which causes them the least inconvenience. This is not to say, however, that the child is any the worse off for this. This merely echoes the situation of many mothers who don't plan families but who are devoted to their offspring nonetheless when they come along.

In some ways, therefore, the minder can be seen, at least through the child's eyes, as more of a substitute for the mother figure than the nanny who verges on that of teacher as well as big sister. From the mother's perspective, however, the nanny is more of a replica of herself because she can be asked to do most of the things that the mother would have done had she been able to. This cannot be expected of a childminder who has a number of voices to obey and therefore has to do things her own way in the end. From the mother's point of view, therefore, the nanny stands in for her more effectively while, from that of the child, the minder is probably much nearer to his concept of 'mum', or possibly if an older woman is involved, 'gran'. This is by no means universal, however, as many minders conform exactly to mothers' ideas of the figure they would have been themselves if they had not chosen to go out to work. There are obvious pros and cons in both these scenarios but they both merit some reflection before a decision is reached.

You may have some worries about the fact that a childminder has her own children present alongside your child and you may fear that she is always going to give them preferential treatment however hard she tries not to. Offsetting this anxiety is the fact that your child will be getting close to others of a similar age. This will prepare him for the arrival of his own younger siblings and, at the same time, prevent him from being spoilt, overstimulated and indulged, a possibility when an overzealous nanny has sole charge of one young child.

You may also be concerned by the fact that while a nanny's role is one which takes an active part in the developmental stages of the child and actively encourages the learning process and creativity, the question of minding a child is a much more passive one involving only the basic caring activities of feeding and keeping the child warm and away from harm. Indeed, it could be argued that a childminder probably has too many children to think about to be able to do much other than make sure that the basic creature requirements – warmth, food and shelter – are met. You might also wonder whether, if the time were available, she would have the inclination to do any more than this. It is unlikely, however, that she would have opted for this activity if she did not have a natural affinity with young children and want to do the best she can for them while they are in her care.

The advantages of a childminder

The considerations about the differences between and the strengths and weaknesses of both options are endless but many of them are worth mentioning as they will have different resonances for different people. In any case all the possible implications need to be thought through before a final decision can be reached. If one were to list the advantages of a childminder over a nanny these could include the fact that your own house is immune from the wear and tear and the need to do extra cleaning and tidying, and possibly employ a cleaner, which inevitably comes with having a young child and nanny (and at regular intervals, the local nanny network and their children for coffee mornings). It also means that the mother can come in and out of her own house at will without any fear of causing a major disruption, and even work at home without fear of interruption. This should not be underestimated.

The minder is almost definitely going to be more integrated into the local community than a live-in nanny. This brings all sorts of benefits with it like gaining inside information about the local school; advice about local doctors and dentists; and where to buy the cheapest strawberries. As mentioned earlier, the minder is very likely to be planning to stay in the area for the foreseeable future. Her husband probably works locally and her children may well be at school in the area. It is quite common for one minder to look after a child through to starting school and even beyond. This continuity undoubtedly makes up for any insecurity brought about by the child not being in his own home. Indeed, over a period of years, he will have the added bonus of having two homes in which he feels totally secure and loved.

Related to this last advantage is the fact that the child will become familiar with two probably very different lifestyles which will certainly enrich his early experiences. While his parents are probably dashing around and giving him plenty of quality time, the minder's home may be a more relaxed environment where he can get on with the mundane things of life and not feel under any pressure. The sense of community can also be experienced by the mother when she drops her child off in the morning and bumps into the other mothers who are using the same minder. This can result in a strong network which can act as an important support system for all the mothers in question. They may help each other out by dropping children off and picking them up, for example, when illness or other emergencies strike.

The limitations of the childminder

There are, however, some things which a childminder cannot provide which a nanny can. While these may be deemed unnecessary they nonetheless need to be considered.

Generally speaking there is less flexibility in using a childminder rather than a nanny to care for your child. This manifests itself in a number of different ways but in essence it means that you need to be a very accurate timekeeper if you are working with a minder. Minders look after children from different families, as well as their own, and therefore have to have the confidence that you will arrive to collect your child when you say you will. If your child is at home with your nanny the situation is less urgent if you are delayed. A minder has to know when to put the child's shoes and coat on and tell him that you are on your way. Bad time-keeping makes her tasks unmanageable. She can decide at very short notice that she no longer wants to look after your child if you are behaving badly so it is in your interests to be conscientious. Good childminders are always in short supply so it is worth treading carefully. The morning needs to be highly organised if you are going to get your child to a minder on time and you need to think ahead about such things as the weather and what clothes need to be taken with the child. The minder cannot, like the nanny, pop back for a raincoat if the weather looks threatening later in the day.

The hours during which a minder can look after your child can be fairly restricted for some working parents. Many will accommodate you between eight in the morning and six in the evening. They have their own family life to think of as well, however, and do not want to have extra children around after this time. A few are a little more flexible than this but many are rightly adamant about it. Thus if you cannot get back to pick your child up by say six every day this might prove problematic. Many nannies work on to seven and even beyond if the parents work long hours, as so many do these days. Equally, there is no babysitting and no weekend coverage provided by a childminder. This needs to be found elsewhere and may well involve you in extra expense. A number of private agencies provide a babysitting service if nobody else is available to help out. You are also on your own when it comes to such tasks as caring for your child's clothes and tidying his bedroom. Nursery duties are, of course, way beyond the brief of the childminder.

Where the experience of the child is concerned there are certain limitations (in addition, of course, to many other positive things) in being a member of a group in somebody else's home. Inevitably a minimum of individual attention is possible, although this is more than compensated for by the interaction with the other children. It's not possible for the minder to take the children on adventurous outings as her routine is probably fairly rigid and she cannot easily transport so many children about. Coffee mornings with other minders are not common either. Equally it's not easy for a minder to accommodate other activities for individual children such as dancing or piano lessons. Instead the children have to accompany the minder when she undertakes her daily chores such as shopping and going to the bank and, in the home, have to play their part in cleaning and tidying the house. This can be seen, in many ways, as a more exact imitation of what a child would be doing with its own mother in its own home, a fact which many mothers find desirable and reassuring. Unlike the nanny who usually concentrates much more on education and stimulus, the minder is necessarily more concerned with getting through the day as efficiently and cheerfully as possible. For many mothers this is considered to be what is required: a true mirror of real life.

For the child the other children in the group are the ones with whom he will develop social relationships, whether he likes it or not. His social life will be less open-ended than the one experienced with a nanny. For the mother the main problem is likely to be the lack of time in which to have an extended conversation with the minder about the way things are going. They will only meet for very short periods of time and probably never be present together with the child except at hand-over time. This can be a cause of anxiety for the mother and needs to be considered.

All in all there are a number of significant ways in which employing a childminder differs from employing a nanny, from the parents', the carer's and from the child's perspectives. The nanny and the minder play different roles and, where the mother is concerned, make different demands of her. There is nothing ultimately to say whether these differences are inherently better or worse and, in any case, individuals vary so enormously that it is impossible to say that a minder is better than a nanny or vice versa. There are as many good, bad and middling nannies as there are minders and indeed parents. What needs to be considered carefully, however, is how the essential differences will affect a particular family situation, financially, practically and emotionally. It may well be that, on balance, the childminding option is, for a variety of reasons, deemed the most appropriate choice. If that is the case then the next task is to make contact with a minder and establish a relationship with her as soon as possible.

Employing a childminder

Finding a minder for your child

As we have already seen the method of employing a childminder differs considerably from that of finding a nanny. The gap between private and public childcare is central to this difference, because, as soon as the question of a child being cared for out of his own home arises, the state provides a framework of legislation to protect the child in question. It is illegal, for example, for somebody who is not registered with her local authority to look after a child under the age of eight for pay and for more than two hours in her own home. A system of registration operates, therefore, in all areas and there is somebody employed by every local authority, at least in principle, to deal with this issue.

It is to that person that the mother in search of a childminder for her child should apply in the first instance. She will usually be given a list of possible minders but, from that point onwards, she is on her own. The next step is to arrange to interview the ones who look most likely from the list (geographical proximity will be a criterion of selection in this situation) and to come to a decision concerning the particular minder she wants to look after her child.

The process of interviewing childminders, like nannies, is

largely a matter of intuition. Much depends on first reactions, especially in this case where it is not just the person one is assessing but also the environment in which the child might well be spending much of his time in the future. It is not simply a question of personal chemistry, therefore, but a much more complex one in which key questions have to be addressed very quickly. On entering someone else's home the mother will ask herself a host of questions: Is it clean? Is there enough room for play? Is it safe? Is it child-friendly? Is there a bit of room outside? Does the dog look friendly? Are there any toys around? First impressions will, most probably, provide instant responses to these almost subliminal questions, providing a basis for the more specific enquiries which she should ask during the course of the interview.

Whether or not you take your child along to the interview depends upon whether you think he will be a hindrance or a help. A young baby may not be the latter, except that you will be able to judge the interviewee's response to him, but an older child will be able to produce reactions to the environment as well, possibly noticing things which passed you by. Some people suggest that ideally two interviews should take place, one in the minder's home and one in your own so that she can get a sense of your domestic standards, and understand your expectations more clearly. This is also a good opportunity for the minder to meet the child's father.

However you decide to conduct the interview there are certain questions which have to be asked and areas which have to be clarified before you can consider taking someone on. Many of these would be part of a nanny interview as well, some are more specific to this situation.

As with a nanny, and indeed perhaps even more so with this option where the mother's degree of control is considerably less, you need to be totally reassured, at the outset of the relationship, that your views on child-rearing and those of the potential minder are totally compatible. While small details may, and probably will, vary you need to be completely happy about the way that your child will be cared for in your absence. To this end the usual questions about diet, discipline, attitudes to things like potty-training, play, television, sweets, and table-manners need to be tackled and answered to your complete satisfaction. If these issues are not raised at this stage it will be more difficult, than with a nanny, to bring them up again. With a minder, it is less a case of telling her what you want, than of finding out what she normally does. If what she does is not to your liking then she is not the minder for you.

Once you have covered these basic areas you need to find out how your child will fit in with this minder's present arrangements. How many children does she look after at present? What age and sex are they? How far away do they live? Does she pick up any children from school? How many children does she have of her own? Who else is usually in the house? It is vital to be able to envisage the group dynamics of the children she cares for and to try and imagine how she organises her day. More importantly you need to know how your child will fit into this scenario. Will he be swamped, overwhelmed or stimulated by other children who will contribute to his own development and sense of well-being? Much of this can only be speculation on the mother's part but it is important for her to find out things such as whether or not there are other people around, for example lodgers, about whom she may be a little worried. Placing your child in someone else's home means that he will have to participate in everything that goes on in that environment, and you need, therefore, to

EMPLOYING A CHILDMINDER

know as much about what goes on inside those four walls as possible.

Very importantly you need to be sure, if you have found your minder through a route other than that of the local authority – an advertisement in a newsagent's window, or on a notice-board at your clinic for instance – that she is registered. If she is not and you feel that she would be ideal for your needs, nonetheless, you can suggest that she becomes registered and thereby a legal childminder. This is not a complicated procedure but it is one which will put everybody's mind at rest. Other things you clearly need to know include the nature of the minder's previous experience. You could ask for the phone number of one of the other mothers she has worked with and do a quick phone check later. Above all, to protect yourself and your child, it is best to agree upon a trial period before you both commit yourselves to each other indefinitely.

You need to be happy, also, about such difficult things as whether you think this minder is going to disrupt your child's language development. Does she, for example, have an accent or pronunciation so different from yours that your child will have difficulty in understanding her or be confused by it? Even more problematically, do you think that there is a danger that your child might be exposed to a set of social or ethical values which are not the ones you hold yourself? (These last two questions could arise when employing a nanny as well, of course.) You need to weigh up all these things in your mind before reaching your final decision.

The final area of discussion in your interview should cover the details of the way in which this minder defines her role and her conditions of work. How does she deal with illness, either her own or that of the child? How do the holidays work out? What does she charge? Does she have an insurance policy which covers injury to your child or damage to her property? Naturally you need to tell her about any special conditions relating to your child in the areas, for example, of diet and health, in addition to simply telling her what he likes and dislikes and the nature of his personality.

There's an enormous amount to get through in an interview with a minder which cannot, realistically, go on for longer than about an hour. Both people involved are assessing each other – the minder has to find out whether or not you would be an easy and pleasant person to work with and vice versa. In the end it's a partnership that's in question. If, finally, all the practical considerations seem unproblematic the mother has to ask herself the fundamental question about whether or not she feels that this person has become a childminder primarily because she needs the extra money or because she enjoys looking after children and is a 'natural' mother. This is a very difficult assessment to make and, in any case, if you feel that all things being equal, this minder could be the right one for your child, a second interview is almost certainly necessary.

Negotiating terms

The local authority often plays another role in the process of a mother and childminder establishing a new partnership and that is in the provision of a standard contract which is sent to all minders on the council's list. Once, therefore, you have come to a decision about the minder with whom you wish now to make a formal arrangement the next stage is for the minder in question to supply the mother with an outline contract which delineates her conditions of service. (It is worth noting that many are not in the luxurious position of being able to choose – many mothers in urban areas are grateful to be able to find one minder who can look after their children.) This demonstrates yet another fundamental difference from employing a nanny where it is the mother who provides the contract and who has the control over the conditions of service it outlines.

The minder's contract will give details about whether or not she expects to be paid when she takes her holiday or when you take your holiday; the hours during which she is prepared to look after your child; what happens if only part of the day is needed, that is, whether she is paid for a full day or pro rata; and it will give a list of her duties. Both parties sign the contract and retain a copy of it.

There is, of course, some room for negotiation outside the basic contract although inevitably less flexibility than with a nanny. A childminder's hours are fairly fixed, few like to work later than six at the very latest as they have their own families to tend to. In addition you need to be clear between yourselves about whether or not the mother will supply the minder with such things as nappies or special items of food. Mothers with very young babies might, for example, want to supply expressed milk in bottles in an attempt to keep breastfeeding going as long as possible. Will the child come along with his own toys and a spare set of clothes? These are the sort of minute details which have to be decided upon, and strictly observed thereafter, as the minder has to deal with a number of mothers all of whom require slightly different arrangements and have subtly different expectations of her. She, in turn, has to juggle all these different requirements and expectations in such a way as to keep everybody relatively happy. This is a demanding responsibility and one to which all the mothers involved should remain sensitive and responsive.

Establishing a relationship

Unlike the mother/nanny relationship, no mother has exclusive rights to her childminder and her demands are just a few of the ones that are continually being made of her. As in nanny-sharing the non-exclusivity of the partnership is fundamental to employing a childminder, but, unlike the former, you are unlikely to be close to the other mothers involved, and you are certainly not in a position to choose them.

In forming a relationship with your childminder time is of the essence and all the communicating needs to be done at breakneck speed when you drop your child off in the morning or pick him up again in the afternoon. The best way of establishing a good working relationship with a childminder is to make as few demands as possible and to adhere to the conditions of the contract as closely as possible. What this means is, unlike the situation with a nanny, the best childminding occurs when the mother and the minder have very little close contact with each other. This results in a situation in which the child knows both of you intimately and depends entirely upon the network that you both create for him but in which you hardly know each other. In fact you may not even enter the minder's home again but merely glimpse it through the front door. You have to accept that what is a familiar environment to your child may be an unknown one to you. This can result in such strange situations as your child knowing exactly what would form an ideal Christmas present for his minder (a glass duck to go with the other glass ducks on the sideboard, for example) while you have no such insights into your 'substitute's' preferences.

The best kind of relationship between a mother and a minder is a professional, working one in which each person plays an equal but complementary role. While a nanny is a mother's employee, in a mother/childminder relationship the former is the latter's client, along with a number of others. It is a fundamentally different form of partnership which, by necessity, must abide by a number of fundamentally different rules.

For the most part, therefore, the mother's best course of action is to respect and trust the minder she works with, be entirely conscientious where time-keeping is concerned and as brief and succinct as possible when communicating with her. While this may sound a little clinical – and of course it goes without saying that the best partners are usually friends as well – it is much more a formula for success than if the mother keeps hanging around the minder's door to see what's going on, phoning up to check on things, and arriving to pick up her child ten minutes late. All the checking should have been done in the early stages and after that the minder should be left as much as possible to get on with her job. Small details such as looking as cheerful as possible, thanking the minder, and generally showing your appreciation for a job well done, go a long way to lightening the latter's load and turning her duties into pleasures. It is likely that your childminder is also a neighbour and therefore your relationship with her will extend naturally into that sphere as well.

Some writers have pointed out that there is likely to be a class difference between childminders and the mothers who use them. Julia Brannen and Peter Moss, for example, state that 'Childminders are mostly working-class and have average or below average levels of education; but many of the mothers whose children they care for are in professional or managerial jobs and have high levels of education. The potential for substantial differences in values, attitude and practice is obvious.' While this is true to a certain extent it is far from universal as the class barriers in this situation are undoubtedly shifting now that more women go back to work for financial reasons. This analysis also fails to point out the enormous advantages for the child, and the enriching experience for the mother, that can come from extending relationships outside one's immediate social group.

As with a nanny, however, the key to sustaining a workable relationship between a mother and a minder consists of effective communication. Thus both partners need to make some space for discussing potential problems before they become full-blown ones. Mothers, for the most part, would like to know how their children have spent their day and this needs to be catered for, in however minimal a way. In addition the mother must tell the minder if, for example, the child is off his food or has gone back to wetting his pants. It's all a question of degree, saying just enough and not too much – a formula which, in the end, comes with practice.

Establishing a routine

As with employing a nanny you learn best how to cope with a childminder by practice. Keys to success include careful organisation on everybody's part. The morning becomes crucial, for instance, as not only do you not have any help in the house to placate a screaming child while you put on your make-up for work, you also have to anticipate the day ahead; decide what clothes your child is going to need later in the day; allow enough time to drop your child off; have a brief chat with the minder; and still negotiate the traffic in time to get to work. It becomes more vital for you to be a car user in these circumstances as depending on public transport can be problematic.

'Handing over' can be as emotional an experience with a minder as with a nanny. The difference with the minder is that she has her own children and other 'deliveries' to cope with as well, and is therefore less well equipped than a nanny to deal with it. Conversely, however, the fact that you are not abandoning your child in his own home can have the effect of diminishing, for him, the emotional side of things. The attraction of a new environment and other children in the minder's home can act as a useful distraction.

Once your child is in the minder's care he passes his day much as he would do if he was at home with his mother, although he is in the company of other children who are not siblings. In some respects, as we have seen, the minder is less flexible than a nanny for going on trips outside the house with her children. Having said that there are, nonetheless, a number of ways in which childminders can slot into an existing network to increase the level of stimulus offered to the children in their care. The local authority plays a role in establishing a network for minders in the form of toy libraries which are set up to allow the children of minders variety in their playthings. It is impossible to expect minders themselves to supply the full range of toys that the different children in their care really need. The local toy library is also a place where minders can meet and chat to each other. This kind of resource is vital to making childminding more than a mere 'passing of time' activity. In some areas minders are organising their own community groups, as in the Battersea Minders' Project, to create a network which will help them enrich their work.

Childminders are in the same position as many mothers with children at home, only with more children to look after than most. Like mothers they can, and frequently do, make use of community activities and joint facilities provided for the under-fives, among them 1 o'clock clubs and playgroups of different sorts. Interestingly, when groups of different carers visit such places the minders tend to mix with the mothers while the nannies cluster together. There are often two cultures operating side by side in these situations, the nannies tending to define themselves as a group of professionals and the minders seeing themselves as mothers earning some extra money by doing what they can do best, namely mothering. Where cost is concerned, however, the distinction between nannies (especially those who work for more than one employer) and childminders is being gradually eroded. This is particularly obvious when a family has more than one child to consider. The cultural difference derives, therefore, less from the rates of pay involved, than from the nanny's training contrasted with the so-called amateurism of the minder. Nannies can be dismissive of childminders and vice versa as they define their tasks in very different ways.

A childminder's flexibility in finding ways of stimulating the children in her care is limited, however, by the fact that she has to juggle a number of different timetables and frequently has to pick up children from school, which means taking all the pre-school children along with her. She also has to do all her own family's shopping and her own household tasks in the course of the day, which restricts the time available to her. In addition much of her time is spent preparing food, undoing and doing up buggies, taking clothes off and putting them on, and making sure nobody falls down the stairs. It is an arduous job which goes far beyond the nursery duties outlined for a nanny. In spite of this it is a childcare option which, because of its close resemblance, in many respects, to the situation in which a child would find himself if his mother had stayed at home to look after him herself, has scored many successes to date.

Working with a childminder

Problem areas

The main area of friction in the mother/minder relationship stems inevitably from the former's sense of frustration which derives from not having much say in how her child spends his time, and in not having much time to discuss matters to any level of satisfaction. Mothers who use minders have to add the word 'frustration', therefore, to the other emotions that all working mothers experience, thereby compounding the problems of returning to work after childbirth. Like the others, however, frustration is an emotion which can be partially dealt with by being recognised and understood for what it is – always the first step in any kind of therapeutic cure.

It is important, for example, to understand why you cannot have the complete control over a minder's activities that you would sometimes like. This stems, in essence, from the fact that the minder could never fully meet the different, and often conflicting, demands of the diverse clients who use her and therefore she has to end up by doing things her way. In addition she has brought up her own children in this manner and sees no problem in doing the same things with the children she looks after. Lacking any professional training in childcare she inevitably uses her own experience and instincts as a basis for her actions. This leaves the mother feeling powerless and maybe useless, which in turn reinforces her feelings of guilt. Not only can she not determine the way her child spends his time which is frustrating enough, she also feels more guilty about 'deserting' him in the first place. With a nanny a mother can feel that she is still performing a role of some kind by establishing the framework within which her child is looked after which is as near as possible to the ideal way in which she would like him to be looked after. With a childminder the mother frequently has to compromise this ideal, as indeed she also has to do with a shared nanny, to a certain extent. The emotional backlash needs some attention if it is not going to take over her life. But she has to offset this, in her mind, with the advantages she has decided are derived from working with a childminder.

There are, inevitably, countless other practical difficulties and worries attached to using a childminder which are different in nature from those linked to employing a nanny. One area of concern is the largely unseen quality of your child's time with the minder. Whereas, with a nanny you can, with warning and within reason, walk into your own house at any point in the day and simply observe what is going on, you cannot do this with a childminder. This may leave a mother with the nagging feeling that anything could be going on out of her vision. In the irrational frame of mind of so many new mothers who experience some level of trauma when leaving their child in somebody else's care for the first time, this fear can grow to enormous proportions and become almost uncontrollable.

The only solution to this is to be as sure as you can be

before you take on a particular childminder that you have picked the right one, and to watch carefully (although not obsessively) for any signs of disturbed behaviour in your child. In the vast majority of cases mothers' complaints centre around the 'too many sweets', 'too much television', and 'too few vegetables' variety and can easily be resolved by a discreet word with the minder. At worst, a change of minder may be necessary if things have gone too far and there are no signs of change in the offing.

A more serious problem is the question of the group dynamics of the children who are looked after by the same minder. The number of children, and combination of ages of the children, is fairly well controlled by legislation, better in fact than in some nanny-share situations in which too many very young children are put together. But no form of legislation can cover the combination of personalities. This is very much a question for the childminder to keep an eye on and, indeed, it is not in her interest to have a group of children who are constantly fighting with each other. What is less easy to spot is whether one child is being bullied by another as this may take place behind the minder's back, for instance, when she is preparing the lunch.

A childminder may not be as busy watching the dynamics of the children in her care as a trained nanny or nursery nurse. She may be more concerned with, say, getting to the bank before it shuts. But this is not always the case and anybody with good mothering skills – however one defines that vague term – will be alert to the well-being of all the children in her care and will notice anything which seems untoward. The main problem comes back, yet again, to the lack of time for adequate communication between mothers and minders. Julia Brannen and Peter Moss discovered from their research, however, that in addition to lack of time, there was actually a reluctance on the part of many mothers to talk over things with their childminder for fear of 'rocking the boat'. They write that 'Particular features of the childcare situation in Britain inhibit fuller communication. The limited choice of childcare must inevitably enter the judgment of any mother deciding whether or not to raise an issue'. Pressures such as these make it even more vital that communication does take place, especially for the sake of the child.

As in nanny-shares the number of people involved in the childcare arrangement with a childminder means that any detour from normality or routine makes the situation difficult. The question of special diets, for example, is particularly hard for a childminder to cope with as it is hard enough cooking for a number of children of different ages at the best of times. Having to shop for, plan, and cook vegetarian meals for one child, and not for the others, can make things split at the seams and become totally unworkable.

A child's illness is also a much greater problem with a childminder than with a nanny for a number of reasons. For one thing it would be quite unfair to pass any illness around the other children in the group if it could be avoided, and, for another, taking a sick child out of his bed to another house where he can't go to bed whenever he wishes to, is unfair and foolish. Mothers who use minders have, therefore, to make contingency plans for the moment when that inevitable illness strikes, whether a bad cold or a bout of chickenpox. This may involve family, friends, neighbours or an understanding employer, but it needs to be thought out at the outset. Where childminders' illnesses are concerned, back-up arrangements have often been made with other minders who are prepared to step into the breach. The Social Services might be able to come to the rescue in this situation but there is no guarantee of this.

All in all, as with the nanny, many of the problems that can arise through using a childminder can be resolved through discussion and through two people respecting and trusting each other. Childminders who take their job very seriously (and large numbers of them do) go as far as setting one evening of the week aside to talk things over with all their clients. This allows all tensions and frustrations to be aired and creates a social network at the same time. Equally the park at the weekend can provide an ideal milieu for a chat and an exchange of views. In the end it is both partners' commitment to making it work that makes it work and, indeed, there are many mothers who would not change their childminder for the world.

The fact that economic necessity on the one hand, and lack of state nursery provision on the other, highlight the childminder so strongly is only part of the picture. Childminders allow mothers who want to, or need to, to return to work; the job provides an income for other mothers who cannot, or do not want to exchange the home for the workplace; and lastly, but most importantly, minders provide a sense of community combined with the next best thing to an ordinary, mother-oriented home life for large numbers of pre-school children. It is a service which demands greater recognition, support, and increased resources as it is undoubtedly among the most desirable childcare options for many families in the 1990s.

While the most vociferous working mothers' campaign aims to obtain the same sort of state protection when employing a nanny as one has when taking on a childminder, in the case of the latter there is pressure being put on government to increase the protection of standards.

This is to be done through the introduction of childminding courses run by local authorities and the standardisation of the minimum criteria for becoming a childminder. With this kind of improved back-up this option would become more desirable, effective and useful.

PART 4

The day nursery

Assessing the day nursery

Unlike many other countries in Europe which have a highly developed system of state-run day nurseries which exist specifically to look after the children of working parents, and which play a vital role in the community, Britain has not pursued this childcare option with much enthusiasm or consistency. As a result the vast majority of pre-school day nurseries which do exist are run either privately or by voluntary groups. This means that it is difficult to ensure that a standard of care is maintained throughout this sector, and inevitably there is much variation in the type and quality of nursery care available. While this increases choice it makes selection difficult and hazardous as well as enormously dependent upon the location in which you live. Consistency of standards (in spite of the vital role of the local authority in providing guidelines and regular inspections) is as lacking as that of provision itself, and much care must be exercised in choosing a day nursery for your child. What does exist has evolved in an ad hoc manner in response to growing market demands rather than as a result of a planned system of controlled care.

The lack of cheap and widely accessible care in this sector has undoubtedly led to the expansion of the nanny/mother's help/childminder alternatives which are much more widespread in this country than elsewhere in Europe. Britain has opted for a laissez-faire approach towards the care of children of working parents, and left the choices and assessment of standards largely in their hands. The day nursery, in its various guises, is nonetheless one of the options on offer and one which deserves serious attention from the working parent of the 1990s.

Until recently the day nursery was an elitist institution where children of wealthy parents went to get ahead with their education. Today, after childminders, such nurseries provide the most popular form of pre-school childcare for working parents in this country. Recent research shows, for example, that while roughly a quarter of all women with pre-school children and full-time jobs use childminders (relations and friends provide well over half the total childcare needed in this context) about a tenth of them send their children to day nurseries. This is a larger proportion than the one which opts for a nanny. In fact, more than 44,000 children attended full daycare nurseries in the early 1990s.

What these figures don't tell us, however, is that it is much harder to find a place for a very young child in a day nursery than it is to locate one for a child who is two years old or over. While this situation is changing quite rapidly as we speak (especially in the private sector where it is clear that there is a market demand to be met) it is still far from widespread. A quick survey of day nurseries in the London Borough of Wandsworth, for example, gives a clear indication of the numbers of them which will take in very small children. Out of a list of 130 nurseries provided by the Wandsworth Social Services Department only seventeen take children under two years of age at the time of writing. Of them, one takes children at eighteen months; ten take them at a year old; one at six months; two at three months;

and only two from birth. The last five in question consist of an Art Centre crèche, two workplace nurseries and two community nurseries. No council nurseries or private nurseries in Wandsworth take children under the age of two. While Wandsworth is probably among the best served London boroughs where numbers of day nurseries are concerned, it is clear, nonetheless, that it generally fails to provide childcare for working mothers of very small children.

One of the reasons for this gap, as for so many other components of this complex picture, is financial. Children under the age of two are expected to have a greater ratio of nursery staff to children – one to three, to be precise, as opposed to one to four for children between the ages of two and three, and one to eight for children aged between three and five. It is more costly, therefore, to provide a nursery service for very young children and this is probably a key reason why there is so much reluctance to do so. This is undoubtedly combined with the fact that, when there is little financial incentive to decide otherwise, many mothers feel that their very young children are best looked after in their own home, and indeed that a live-in nanny provides a much more flexible option.

Nursery daycare for very young children is therefore thin on the ground. It becomes increasingly widespread, however, for children over the age of one and even more so for those over the age of two. This varies according to the kind of day nursery in question, whether one is considering a council-run nursery, a workplace, a private or a community nursery. Each model has its own approach, and its own advantages and disadvantages, but before they are considered in turn it is worth thinking a little more about the question of what nurseries in general have to offer the working parent with a pre-school child.

*

While it has been shown that nurseries are not widely available for very young children, employers and groups of parents themselves are making some headway on this front with the result that more and more provision of this sort is becoming available. In the first instance the day nursery provides a similar caring environment to that of a childminder in that it is situated out of the child's home and the care in question is shared with other pre-school children. Nurseries, however, employ trained staff (NNEB or similar) for the most part and have the advantage of being able to provide a wide range of play equipment and a much more planned routine of play, learning and visits. Both options help children develop their social skills to a high level but, in the context of a nursery, these skills are often developed in a more active and educational framework. At a day nursery, for example, there is little risk of children being put in front of a television for hours on end; they are less likely to be given sweets; taken around the supermarket, or left to their own devices for long periods of time – all situations which *may* arise when the childminder in question is not up to standard. Needless to say, a childminder can also offer a stimulating environment, something which is particularly desirable for the older pre-school child, but some parents may feel happier that the developmental stages are being closely monitored by carers who are trained in this respect. If you are considering putting a baby into a private day nursery, it is vital that you visit a number of them, and make sure that the staff in question are trained and that the routine is an acceptable one for your child.

All nurseries must be registered with their local Social Services Department, and are inspected at regular intervals. It will examine, among other things, the space available;

the safety of the environment in question; the ratio of staff to children; and the number of toilets in relation to the number of children admitted. In addition to providing a set of regulations, based on the Children Act of 1989, the government also provides guidelines for 'good childcare practice' which local authority assessors of nurseries are expected to bear in mind. These include recommendations that the day's programme should be planned before the children arrive; that activities should be appropriate to a child's age and development; that the children should have as many stimulating learning opportunities as possible; that there should be time and space for both quiet and noisy activities; that children should be allowed to work at their own pace; that corporal punishment is illegal; that there should be affection and sensitive responsiveness between the adults and children; that the parents' input should be respected and that there should be a first aid box and training available.

If implemented by a trained childcarer, caring and sensitive guidelines such as these will undoubtedly ensure the quality childcare that is needed to eliminate the inevitable anxiety felt by most parents on handing their child over to a nursery. Some parents think it more likely that the trained carer will see the full implications of, and reasons behind, these guidelines and be able to implement them in a sensible way. They prefer the nursery to the childminder for this reason.

Considerations relating to the choice of a nursery for a young child include its hours of opening and its location. The latter will depend on what kind of nursery is in question – workplace or other. It is a central factor in determining many people's choices in this area. Increasingly nurseries are open for a period of time which allows working parents with a conventional nine-to-five timetable to make use of them. There is a great deal of pressure, also, being applied by groups such as the Pre-School Playgroups Association, for playgroups which hitherto only offered part-time childcare to move into full day care. In 1989, for instance, only 600 such groups offered this kind of service whereas by 1991 that figure had risen to over 1,000. Of the 130 Wandsworth nurseries mentioned above, for example, 37 are open long enough to accommodate the needs of working parents. The most common hours are 8am to 6pm, although a very small number stay open for longer. (Probably the most accommodating of all in this respect is the Blackshaw Nursery at St George's Hospital in Tooting which stays open between 7am and 10pm to help workers on shifts.) This means that only parents with regular nine-to-five working hours can make use of most day nurseries. While this fulfils the needs of many there are clearly others whose working hours are longer, or more irregular, and they cannot make use of this option easily.

In this respect this form of childcare provides the same kind of restriction as the childminder who will rarely work flexible hours. It means that parents have to find a nursery which is as near to home or work as possible and that they will find it difficult to participate in any aspect of their job which falls outside the nine-to-five day. In addition, nursery hours have to be respected absolutely. At the end of the day the staff want to return to their own lives and homes, and do not want to hang on waiting for a tardy mother to pick up her child. This can put tremendous pressure upon a working mother, especially when she has to negotiate busy and unpredictable urban traffic on her journeys to and from work.

Clearly nurseries are of no assistance when it comes to evenings and weekends. All help for those times has to be found elsewhere. For the most part, though, nurseries only close down for a couple of weeks' holiday in the summer, in addition to bank holidays. On the whole, though, they can only provide a childcare solution in a situation in which the parents concerned can cope with a fixed and regular routine.

Where cost is concerned the nursery option presents parents with an enormous variation of possibilities. From a completely free place in a council nursery (a very rare phenomenon) to an expensive place in a private day nursery (anything up to £200 a week in London), the cost of nursery care varies dramatically depending upon the kind of nursery in question and the area in which it is located. It is not necessarily the case that the most expensive is the best, however, as a certain amount of social status can be attached to a child being sent to a particular nursery while a much cheaper one may well provide care of equal quality.

The more crucial question relating to the cost of nursery care, where a baby or young child is concerned, is the comparison with employing a nanny in the child's own home. Nurseries are, on the whole, cheaper than trained nannies – averaging at the time of writing something between £40–£100 a week depending on the hours in question and whether or not they are subsidised. It should also be remembered, however, that the cost for nursery care is per child and that two or more small children at a nursery could prove to be an expensive option. The average cost of a nursery tends to be a little higher than a childminder. The comparison here, where quality is concerned, is between trained and untrained care, but for some the instincts of a childminder may be thought to outweigh the formal training of an NNEB trained nanny or nursery nurse, at least where a very young child is concerned. As with all things, therefore, weighing up the pros and cons of a nanny, nursery or childminder is not simply a matter of finances but also one in which personal childcare preferences play an important part.

The question of cost and the quality of care at any one individual nursery are not the only things to take into account, however. It is worth, also, thinking about the fact that, possibly unlike a nanny, a nursery is a stable form of care. Nurseries come and go much less frequently than nannies (although the turnover of staff inside them needs careful watching) and they can, therefore, be a form of birth-to-five childcare for many children. This level of stability is clearly one of the nursery's most attractive features. In addition staff illness is less of a problem as there is always an immediate back-up system present. This means that you can rely on nurseries in a way that you cannot always depend on a nanny who is much less easy to replace when ill. As far as children's illnesses are concerned, however, it is unfair to send an ill child to a nursery (as with a childminder) where he will rapidly infect all his peers. This almost certainly means a day off work for the mother if there are no helpful relations or friends around.

The combination of stability, reliability and its strong place within the local community (with the exception of the workplace nursery) are all positive features in favour of the day nursery. To these can be added the strong social education that is available to nursery children and the wonderful preparation for school that it provides. This is, perhaps, where the nursery scores over the nanny, although, once again, the question of group care versus individual attention needs to be taken into account. While a nanny can often devote herself to the care and education of a single young child, nursery children never get less than one in three attention and it is always possible that their individual requirements could be neglected. In a day nursery, as in a nanny-share, a nursery nurse could be looking after three children under the age of two, a rare situation in the context of a nanny employed by a single family unit.

Perhaps the greatest worry about putting a very young child into a nursery is that he will become institutionalised as a result of not being looked after in a natural home situation, whether it is his own home with a nanny, or that of a childminder. There is indeed strong cultural resistance to this in Britain (much more so than in Continental Europe) along with a widespread, subconscious fear that the child's emotional development will be impaired by being cared for out of the context of the home. Some writers maintain that it is much better to put a child into a nursery before the age of six months as he will be less resistant at that point to a strange environment and to strange people than he will be during the next few months of his life. It is preferable, also, that the baby or toddler enters a nursery gradually, getting to know his new companions by visiting them on a number of gradually extended occasions. This clearly has to be done while the mother is still on maternity leave as it would be impossible once she returns to work. It is vital, also, that parents let the nursery staff know about their children's routine, how and when they like to sleep, what they prefer to eat, what their responses are, and things like their favourite toys. This is just one aspect of the essential system of communication that parents and nursery staff must enter into to ensure that the child will be cared for properly.

In the end, however, the question of the ratio of staff to children in day nurseries is the key to their effectiveness or otherwise. Very young children require close individual attention. There has to be time to cuddle a child who is upset; to pick up a child who falls over; and to ensure that each child gets enough help at meal times and enough stimulus through the day. At the same time even the youngest child benefits from a social situation and reaps rewards from the company of other children who are older, younger or of the same age. In a nursery environment preschool children can mix freely with each other. As Marion Kozak has written in an essay in *Daycare for Kids*:

> Both for younger and older children being in a group is a welcome experience. Babies watch the toddlers as if enchanted while the older ones playact and imitate adult relationships and develop caring and affectionate personalities. This is very much the pattern of those cultures where older siblings are given charge of the younger ones, similar to the way families used to be brought up in Europe before the demise of the extended family.

In the very best nursery environments this interaction will be encouraged by trained staff who understand the benefits to be gained for all the children concerned, and who are committed to ensuring that this takes place.

The balance of the need for individual attention against the benefits of early socialisation is a difficult one to assess in the abstract and will depend upon the personality of each individual child. An introverted child, for instance, may well benefit from being part of a group. Parents do not, of course, ever have to opt for only one solution. Many favour employing a nanny for the early months and moving on to a nursery a little later. The need for security and stability does not mean that no changes can be accommodated, indeed change can be a positive thing and children cannot be entirely protected from it. It is a question, rather, of how transitional stages are handled and how to meet the need for a child to have a secure underpinning to his life, even if it is only the regularity of spending the evenings and weekends with his parents.

One thing is certain about day nurseries and that is that they are in short supply, at least, that is, the financially more accessible ones. There is still much to be done in this country to make availability more widespread if we are to begin to match the provision in Continental Europe. Most nurseries of all kinds have waiting lists and cannot fulfil the demand for places. As a result parents are thrown back on to nannies if they can afford them, or childminders if they can't. A carefully monitored, accessible nursery system has still to be developed in this country. While nannies are not subject to inspection and childminders are not trained in childcare, the sensible middle path – the day nursery – seems the logical way forward and one which, if widely available, many parents would welcome.

Finally there is no evidence from research to suggest that children's development suffers in any way from their being brought up in a nursery from an early age. Some reports, in fact, such as one put out by the Social Affairs Unit in September of 1992, entitled *Families in Dreamland*, go as far as to suggest that, 'Children placed in day nurseries are intellectually and socially more advanced than toddlers cared for at home and show no signs of emotional disturbance.' There seems to be no conclusive evidence that a child who is looked after in daycare from an early age is disadvantaged in any way, and it is clear that, as long as quality care is ensured, a child is served just as well by daycare as by mothercare.

Council and community nurseries

If both a nanny and a childminder are childcare options which are out of reach financially for working parents, and no free care, in the form of friends or relatives is available either, then the only possibility is to look for a subsidised place in a council nursery, or a relatively cheap place in a community nursery which is itself subsidised in one way or another.

In this country this situation is not an enviable one to be in, however, as Britain does not invest as much money in pre-school childcare as do other European countries such as Sweden, Denmark, Finland and France. Nevertheless such places do exist, albeit in very small numbers, although their availability will vary depending upon the area in which you live and the policy of your local authority towards pre-school childcare. The money given by central government for these purposes is administered by the local Social Services Department, as indeed are the day nurseries which are funded by this means. The way of finding out about such places, therefore, is to contact your local Social Services and ask for details.

It should be pointed out, however, that places in local

authority-run nurseries are extremely limited – less than two per cent of under-fives in this country have a place in a council nursery – and that they are unlikely to be allocated unless certain needy conditions are met by the parents and child in question. The criteria for need will, however, vary to some extent from area to area. While some local authorities will give places to children of single parents, others will give priority to children of low income families; to physically or mentally-handicapped children; or to children who are considered to be at risk because, for example, they have a parent who is known to be violent. So few in number are places at council-run nurseries that only special cases like these can be accommodated, and even if these conditions are met, there is no guarantee of an immediate place being available. Many children in great need remain on waiting lists for some time. In addition children under the age of two are rarely admitted into council nurseries.

Council nurseries vary from area to area but they are usually open between the hours of 8am and 6pm and offer places on a part-time or full-time basis. When it is a question of real need, a very few places are free, but most are means-tested so that some contribution is required from parents. Some nurseries of this kind sell places to less needy parents or to local employers who want to provide childcare in their locality.

The staff are usually qualified nursery nurses and the Social Services Department takes responsibility for regular checks on safety, hygiene, and the nature of the staffing and staff/children ratios. Lack of funds usually means that staffing is at a minimum. Inevitably standards vary from place to place and there exist some very high quality council nurseries with highly dedicated, hardworking staff. The sadness is that there aren't more of them available to all those people who could benefit from them. It is, in fact, the only area of childcare which has shrunk in size over the years – from being available to 17 per cent of pre-school children in 1948 to only three per cent in 1984. It has decreased again since then.

The wide regional variations in council nursery availability are also significant. There are, for example, no such nurseries in Barnsley, Rotherham or Dudley, or in the counties of Cornwall, Wiltshire, West Sussex, Shropshire or Warwickshire. By contrast in the London boroughs of Islington and Camden six per cent of under-fives attend a council nursery; in Brent the figure is five per cent. In Manchester it is four per cent. You lose your right to a place if you move from one area to another.

The special conditions that inevitably surround council nurseries in this country mean that they remain at the periphery of the childcare discussion, still confined to the arena of the under-privileged. They are not seen as a right by more fortunate parents who can afford their own private childcare and who have little interest in the state sector. It is important, though, to understand that the dominant forms of pre-school childcare for working parents in this country – childminders, private nurseries and nannies – are so widespread compared with other countries in Europe because of the absence of a system of state-subsidised and state-run care which, in contrast, is highly developed in a number of countries across the Channel. If this gap were filled and the state provided a system of care for pre-school children of working parents there would undoubtedly be a significant change in the attitude towards such care and much less cultural resistance towards it. This in turn would help to ease much of the guilt and unease which presently surrounds this area where the working mother is concerned.

Community, or voluntary, nurseries are one way in which attempts have been made to bridge the private/public divide in the British childcare system, a divide which makes so many of the discussions about options come down to a question of economics rather than one about the benefits of one form of childcare over another. These nurseries have been initiated by users for the most part, inasmuch as they have often been set up by groups of parents who were unable to find any alternative form of childcare available to them. They are usually there to serve a particular locality, be it a council housing estate or a defined community or district. Sometimes communities linked through attendance of a particular church have banded together to create such a facility for their children, although access is frequently made available to others outside the immediate grouping.

The special characteristics of community nurseries relate both to the way in which they are funded and in which they are managed. Most are subsidised in some way or another, whether by the state, by a charity or by an employer and, as a result, are generally cheaper than private nurseries which are usually organised as small businesses. The local community plays a role in managing these nurseries and thereby contributes to policy decisions and to the way in which they are run. They are also, unlike the council nurseries, open to all children in the community and operate, usually, on a first-come, first-served waiting list scheme. As ever demand for these cheaper childcare options outstrips supply and the lists are often fairly long.

Community nurseries have grown in number over the last decade and now play a significant role in certain areas. Notable examples which have filled enormous local needs include the Tottenham Green Under-Fives in Harringay, which takes children between the ages of two and five, and the Ackroyd Community Nursery in Lewisham which takes children from 18 months up to school age, in addition to running a number of out-of-school schemes. It also has a baby unit which takes children between three and 18 months which is in a family house.

In Sheffield the Manor Community Nursery takes 12 children from parents who live on the Manor Estate. This nursery is entirely managed by the people who use it, with some help being given by local community workers. The model provided by this scheme is one which many other groups throughout the country are attempting to emulate as, where lower income families are concerned, it is the only way of circumventing the lack of council provision in this area. Furthermore, community nurseries don't have the same stigma attached to them as many council nurseries, and the links between staff and parents are often significantly stronger.

Of the efforts that are currently being made to initiate new daycare ventures of this kind more than half are in London and the South East; 13 per cent are in the West Midlands; and only a small proportion are in the rest of the UK. Community nurseries and partnerships between community and workplace nurseries are both demonstrating this pattern of growth. Most of them are relatively small, catering for something between 11 and 20 children. Only a very small number cater for as many as 40 children.

Where working women in the low income situation are concerned, therefore, childcare choice is fairly restricted but there is a growing awareness, nonetheless, of the expansion of need in this area and many attempts are being made to address it. Inevitably funding is the central stumbling block and only once this has been resolved can the question of quality childcare be discussed. The Children Act guidelines are the key to the question of quality in this area.

The strongest argument of all for community nurseries is, of course, their strong role within the local community and the early exposure of children to other children who are likely to remain their friends for some time to come. The fact that children can be integrated into the locality in this way means that they can help establish networks and relationships between families with working parents which would not otherwise be there. In the case of the community nursery this occurs as a result not simply of the parents taking the children to and fro in the mornings and evenings, but also of parents meeting each other in the context of managing the nursery, and being involved with such activities as fundraising and organising social events. This natural extension, and indeed in some cases creation of, a local community is beneficial to children and parents alike and is undoubtedly a strong spin-off of the community nursery concept.

The community nursery idea is still in its infancy at present but, funds permitting, it will undoubtedly continue to play a part in the spectrum of childcare options as it provides professional care; involves parents significantly; plays a role in the community; and has grown up from real necessity rather than simply from someone seeing a gap in the market. It is one of the childcare options that the 1990s will hopefully see expand to its full potential.

Workplace nurseries

Another recently and, until the recession, rapidly expanding form of pre-school childcare is the workplace nursery. At present, however, access is not yet widespread – there are only about 2,000 places available in the United Kingdom in about 300 such nurseries. Given that many new mothers return to work as soon as their statutory maternity leave runs out, that is, at a time when their babies are still highly dependent upon them, there is a great deal of logic in the thought that the best place to look after a baby is as physically near to the mother as possible, that is, at her place of work itself. To a mother who wants to keep breast-feeding her baby as long as possible, this immediately makes sense. She can visit her child during her coffee and lunch-breaks and feel that she is nearby should any problems arise. She doesn't have to wait to get home before she sees the baby either as she can pick him up the moment she finishes work.

This apparently idyllic picture has much to recommend it and is the preferred option for a significant number of working mothers. It is an important option, also, because workplace nurseries take children from a very young age, from as early as three months in many instances. There is, of course, another side to the workplace nursery coin, however. Disadvantages include the trauma of taking a young baby/toddler to work with you every day, possibly through log-jammed traffic or even by public transport. The fact, also, that the baby is so near makes leaving him even more difficult and popping in and out only exacerbates the problem. This close proximity to the child during the day can make it difficult for the mother to make a mental break from him and concentrate fully on the tasks before her. Last but not least, workplace nurseries take a child out of his immediate community and place him in a context in which his peers have only one thing in common with him – that their parents work in the same institution as his mother.

The child is then left without friends in his home community and prevents the mother from becoming a part of the neighbourhood in which she spends her evenings and weekends. Weekend social occasions are more likely, as a result, to be spent with work colleagues than with neighbours, and the child relates to his mother as an employee rather than as a member of a local community. This could clearly present problems when school comes along and peers change overnight.

Another major problem with the workplace nursery concept is the fact that it is almost entirely dependent upon one parent, usually the mother, remaining at the same place of employment for a number of years if the place in the nursery is to be retained. This can put an enormous strain upon a mother who wants to move on but who doesn't want to lose the convenience and stability of the workplace nursery. It may well be that the next employer is not so progressive and doesn't provide childcare of any sort, and it may cause needless disruption for a child who is happy with the existing arrangement.

Clearly the question of job-related childcare needs to be carefully considered if a mother wants to avoid getting caught in this particular trap and finding that she has to stay in a job she has grown to hate, or give up a chance of promotion simply because she doesn't want to disrupt her child's care arrangements. Some employers are considerate enough to guarantee a place even if someone leaves their employ but this may not prove practical if the new job is not in the vicinity.

Workplace nurseries come, therefore, with mixed blessings and should be entered into with forethought as a change in arrangements could mean taking a child completely out of his newly acquired community and throwing him into a kind of limbo where the only world he knows is his mother's place of work. Weighed against these considerations, however, must come the fact that workplace nurseries are usually, although not always, subsidised by various means and therefore not excessively expensive – fees for a single child at the time of writing vary enormously from around £30 to £150 a week. In addition they are a form of professional care, usually to a high standard. They have all the usual advantages and disadvantages of nurseries in general – group dynamics versus individual attention and so on – and they are undoubtedly one of the vital means of providing accessible childcare for working mothers.

The workplace nursery concept has developed in recent years as a response to many companies' growing awareness of their long-term dependence upon their female workforce. They know that school-leavers are less and less available, and that it is a waste to train a woman in a specific job and then to lose her from the workforce once she has had children. It made sense, therefore, to a number of employers – especially those who employed a lot of women; had space on the premises; and demonstrated a level of social responsibility (educational establishments and hospitals unsurprisingly led the way) – to provide childcare for their employees on their premises or nearby. Help came in the last few years in the form of a tax incentive to employers to provide assistance for working mothers. Not all who took action chose to open their own nursery, however. Some bought into places in existing nurseries, others collaborated with local community nurseries, while others provided childcare vouchers which mothers could use however they wished.

Oxfam, for example, has a workplace nursery at its Oxford headquarters but found that a similar solution was not a viable option for its staff in the rest of the country. Instead it opted for a childcare allowance which is open to permanent employees of both sexes who have children under five. Its policy states:

> A childcare allowance is provided as a cost-effective part of Oxfam's policy of equal opportunities in employment. The main purpose of the allowance is to help women already employed by Oxfam to return to work after maternity leave, when they might be otherwise unable to do so because of the costs of providing childcare.

Many have opted for a nursery, however. The Midland Bank, for instance, played a significant role in proposing a widespread system of 300 nurseries which it planned to subsidise. A number of other large companies – among them Thomas Cook which established a 50 place, £35 a week childcare unit at its Peterborough headquarters; British Telecom and Boots – have made important strides forward in this area, although the recession has regrettably modified these good intentions. Some companies have grouped together to form a single centre. The Kingsway

Nursery in central London, set up in 1977, for instance, was jointly funded with money from employers, trade unions and the local authority. Six employers use its facilities and it caters for 36 children between the hours of 8.30am and 5.45pm. In this instance the parents pay a third of the fee and the rest is paid by the employers.

The West Lambeth Health Authority similarly runs two workplace nurseries which cater for employees in a general catchment area. In this case they serve the Tooting Bec, Southwestern, and St Thomas's Hospitals, as well as the clinics and community health centres which are in the area. Initiated in 1989 in Stockwell, one of the schemes provides, at the time of writing, places for 50 children (35 of which are for under twos) on a site opposite St Thomas's Hospital but even this fails to meet the enormous demands from parents working in West Lambeth. The authority ensures that parent-users are involved with much of the decision making that goes on at their centres and the long opening hours, 7am to 10pm, are an attempt to cover as many shifts as possible. A further project being planned by this progressive health authority is in partnership with J. Sainsbury. Together they have provided a 30-place nursery in Streatham, 20 of which have been taken by the health authority. Sainsbury has provided the site.

The Civil Service has nurseries in Hertford, Sunningdale, Central London, Farnborough, Croydon, Swindon and Bootle. Two other well known workplace nurseries are those jointly provided by newspaper employers in Fleet Street and the BBC (the White City Nursery). The former was set up by the newspaper unions in 1986 and was funded by the GLC to provide childcare places for the employees of companies in the locality. They were taken up by Reuters, which has the greatest number of children there; London Weekend Television, and the Guardian Newspaper. The nursery employs six NNEB trained nursery nurses, a cook, a cleaner and a part-time accountant. It takes a total of 26 children at any one time. The unsubsidised cost for a single child is £135 a week, at the time of writing, and it takes children from the age of three months. Most places are subsidised by the employers in one way or another, however. The Fleet Street Nursery operates between the hours of 8am and 6pm and monthly management meetings are held at which parents are present. Parents also participate on the management board of the nursery and generally feel very much part of the whole operation. They are free to come and go as they please, and frequently come in to feed the smaller babies.

The BBC nursery is another example of the way in which employers, unions, parents, voluntary organisations and local authorities can work together in this area. It became a reality after a great deal of parent pressure made the problem a visible one. A number of female BBC employees commissioned an external report and organised a petition. The unions made contact with the relevant local authorities and when the BBC moved to White City, space for a purpose-built nursery became available. It has a 65-place capacity and is open from 8am to 8pm. Places are allocated on a first-come, first-served basis and fees begin at 15 per cent of basic salary up to a maximum of the real cost of a place.

Increasingly, also, private nurseries are being established in commercial centres for use by employees and local residents. All these nurseries, especially the subsidised ones, are characterised by the fact that they are hard to get into and waiting lists are the norm. Fees vary enormously, as we have seen, but for more than one child they can be an expensive proposition.

The main advantages of a workplace nursery are its proximity to work and its reliability. No extra journeys to and from work are entailed, and there are no problems of sickness where the carer is concerned. The usual difficulties are present when the child is ill, however, especially as it involves taking him a significant distance from his own home. Workplace nurseries employ trained, caring staff and provide a fully professional childcare system. Parents are usually involved as much as possible and are frequently encouraged to take an active role in the running of the nursery.

This form of childcare is presently being given special emphasis and encouragement by a number of voluntary organisations, among them the Working Mothers Association and the Daycare Trust. They, and others, see it as an important way forward as it is of benefit not only to parents but also to employers who need to think about the advantages of women coming back into the workforce. By persuading employers of the long-term financial benefit to them, they feel a number of different interests can be catered for at the same time. It is also clearly the way in which the Conservative Government sees the future of childcare in Britain, at least where its tax laws are concerned. The fact, for example, that women who work and employ nannies are being taxed twice does not seem to interest them. There is one anomaly in its tax incentive scheme for employers in this area, however, and it is that employees are taxed on the childcare benefits they receive from their employers. The Workplace Nurseries Campaign is presently working hard to overturn this.

The impact of the recession of the early 1990s upon the envisaged expansion of workplace nurseries is clearly visible, however, and while progress will certainly be made in this decade it will probably not be on the ambitious scale that was imagined only a few years ago.

Private day nurseries

At present there are something like 30,000 places available in private day nurseries in this country. Between 1985 and 1988 just under 500 new nurseries were formed in Great Britain, most of them privately-run, thereby making this type of daycare an extremely popular option for large numbers of working parents.

As has been stated already, however, the vast majority of these places are available to children between the ages of two and a half and five. This means that private day nurseries are often viewed by working parents as an option which follows on from some other form of childcare such as a nanny. It may also be used alongside such an arrangement if nursery attendance is on a part-time basis only. Alternatively it may follow an extended absence from work on the part of the mother. Lastly, some private day nurseries will take children from an earlier age, though this is the exception.

Private day nurseries are run as businesses and therefore respond to market demands. They have to be seen by prospective clients as much as profit-making institutions as ones which provide quality childcare for their offspring. A balance between these two aims is partially ensured by the fact that they all must be inspected at regular intervals by the Social Services. They also have to meet all the requirements of the local authority, which is in turn informed by the guidelines set out in the Children Act. To this extent, therefore, they are subject to checks and controls in a way which the privately employed nanny is not. What this means is that the children to staff ratio is monitored as are all the facilities provided by the school such as space and number of toilets, and the extent of safety precautions.

As has been mentioned in the section on childminders, however, this checking system does not extend to the nature of the care in question. This is left for parents to vet and make decisions about. The largest element of a private nursery's costs is the salary bill for staff. It is vital, therefore, to check that these institutions are not attempting to keep their costs down by employing too many young, inexperienced staff who command lower salaries than ones with a few years' experience under their belts. Fees for private day nurseries are not low especially for those which have a specific educational approach. In London, for example, at the time of writing full-time costs start at about £50 a week but they are frequently double that and more.

When choosing a private day nursery for your child it is recommended that you view several and that you return to them at different times of the day. Like all the other kinds of nurseries described in this section, private nurseries employ nursery nurses with the usual NNEB, and other, qualifications. There are a significant number which follow a particular approach to the education of very young children, such as that put forward by Dr Maria Montessori at the turn of the century, and these will employ nursery nurses who have had this specialised form of training in preference to others. Montessori nurseries stress a graded form of development and give each child a 'key worker' to watch and assess his individual development. Much emphasis is put upon painting, dancing and touch. Many parents like this approach as they can clearly see their children moving through developmental stages. Others feel that it is over-programmed and over-structured for very young children.

Where the over-twos are concerned the emphasis in the majority of private day nurseries is less upon minding and more upon educating. They are viewed, for the most part, as learning centres which will prepare your child for school. Many, in fact, lead into the private educational system and take children up to the age of eight accordingly. Some parents feel that private nurseries can be a form of 'hot house', forcing small children through educational hoops. These institutions tend to favour school uniform and a high level of discipline. Others are more relaxed in their approach and see play as an important part of the early years curriculum.

Private nurseries are characterised, above all, by their enormous variety. The Social Services Department of your local authority can provide you with a list of the ones in your area, as can the local library. Sometimes the former will also provide a guide as to the emphases in different schools. Wandsworth Borough Council, for instance, provides all parents of small children with a copy of its *Under 8's Directory* which lists all the childcare facilities in the Borough, among them council and private nurseries; preschool playgroups; holiday playcentres; and toddler groups. Under the Nurseries section it lists a large number of private day nurseries, giving such details as whether or not there is disabled access; the name of a contact person; the registration number; and a brief description of what is on offer. One, for example, is described as, 'Private Nursery School. Provides early reading and writing skills, play provision and multi-activities'. Another is described as 'Private Nursery School, teaches reading, writing, art, ballet and music'; another as 'Private nursery which aims to promote the development of the pre-school child through play. Number work, reading and writing is also taught', and yet another as 'Partially Montessori Nursery. Offers French lessons. Has outside play area'. Lastly one 'Offers fun, air, and exercise within a broad cultural framework. Many outings plus daily trips to the park'. From these brief outlines the potential client can get a taste of what is in store for his or her child. They show the special emphases of each institution and make the bewildering array of possibilities a little more decipherable. In the end of course, factors such as price, proximity to home or work and size are also important when decisions are finally made.

Many private day nurseries offer part-time, or sessional, care and are therefore not really available to the full-time working mother, unless there is a back-up childcare system in operation, which makes this kind of option an expensive one. Some mothers manage to juggle part-time work with a nursery or a part-time childminder or nanny-share, with part-time attendance at a nursery. Such arrangements are inevitably complex and take a great deal of managing. For many mothers, however, this effort is worthwhile as it provides what they feel to be the right balance between group and individual care; play and learning; social life and privacy.

The private childcare sector is clearly an expanding one as the demand for it remains high. It is an area which has much to offer but which requires careful vetting on the part of parents. As with any other form of childcare, parents who want to send their child to such a nursery must do their homework before they do so. Once this is done and they are convinced that they are paying for a happy and stimulating environment which offers enough clean and safe space, enough appropriate playthings, and plenty of trained and experienced carers to hand, the child in question will clearly have all the essentials of quality pre-school childcare. Beyond those basic requirements it is down to personal preferences as to what skills you want your pre-school child to acquire, whether it be reading Shakespeare or dancing like Margot Fonteyn. In the end, however, this is just icing on the cake of what constitutes a basic form of quality childcare provided by many of the private day nurseries in existence today.

The idea of the day nursery clearly covers a wide spectrum of options, from, at one end, the local authority special needs nursery, to community and voluntary nurseries, to workplace nurseries, to, at the other end, private day nurseries. Socially, economically and ideologically there is little to unite these institutions into a single definition other than to say that they all provide forms of professional group care, outside the home for pre-school children whose parents are in paid employment. They provide another option – sometimes from birth but more often from the age of two – to employing a nanny, or a childminder. The main advantages of the nurseries is that they are both serviced by professional childcarers and monitored by the state. They clearly provide a very good preparation for school and are both stable and reliable.

For some people these clear advantages are outweighed by the fact that the childminder is a real mother or that with a nanny the child remains within his own home for a much longer period. Where cost is concerned, a day nursery is probably cheaper than a nanny (except when a share is involved) but more expensive than a childminder.

When nurseries are subsidised, whether by the state or by an employer, they can be economically very advantageous. However, when there is more than one child, it could well prove to be the most expensive form of pre-school childcare.

In addition to the full-blown day nursery, other forms of supervised childcare out of the home exist, none of which can, however, provide an adequate form of help for the full-time working mother. But some part-time working mothers can make use of them, as indeed can nannies and childminders.

Some nursery schools for three to five-year-olds exist which are funded by the local authority and usually attached to primary schools. Often these are sessional, morning or afternoon for a couple of hours or so, or they can be full-time from, say, 9am to 3pm. As such they make it possible for a mother to return to work part-time, albeit with enormous restrictions upon her hours of availability.

Crèches, linked most commonly to educational establishments, shopping centres, sports centres, and community centres, are usually temporary or sessional in nature. They rarely make working a possibility but they do enable a mother, nanny or childminder to have some child-free time, whether to pursue an educational or sporting activity or just to go shopping for a couple of hours. While these cannot be said to help the full-time working mother in any way, they nonetheless provide a real source of support for non-working mothers and childcarers.

To return to the idea of the nursery and the concept of it which has changed dramatically over the last decade – initially a place where privileged children went to get a step ahead on the educational ladder, or underprivileged children went to get some quality care – it is now one on which working mothers can rely as a source of professional and reliable childcare. In a decade when the state is spending less and less on the public sector, and in which government money for the under-fives is in shorter and shorter supply, the only significant source of funding for childcare will have to be the private sector. This means that private nurseries will continue to dominate the picture and that employers who can understand the long-term implications of the demographic shifts in the workforce will be the main source of funding for nurseries. We wait to see, in the second half of the 1990s, whether they will take on the mantle of this responsibility and perform this important role to the degree to which it is needed.

PART 5

Caring for the school child

Out-of-school care

Although most discussions about childcare tend to focus on the problems involved in finding care for the pre-school children of working mothers, this does not mean that once those children enter school the problems simply vanish into thin air. On the contrary, because the need for care is no longer a full-time one, the area of part-time childcare has to be confronted along with all the complexities and inconveniences that all forms of part-time work inevitably bring with them. While employing a full-time nanny or childminder is a more expensive undertaking it at least provides somebody with a full-time occupation and income and is therefore relatively easy to arrange, not so out-of-school childcare. Surveys have concluded that 85 per cent of women with children over five who do not work express a wish to do so and many of the 45 per cent of them who currently work part-time would work full-time if childcare were available after school and in the holidays.

Many women decide to go back to work when their children start school either because they need to financially, or because they find the prospect of being in the house alone for much of the day a chilling one. Others feel that five years out of a career is as much as can be tolerated and realise the need to continue a career which was cut short by motherhood. Employers are increasingly receptive to career breaks and realise that it makes long-term financial sense to take trained women back into the workforce after such a break.

The first decision that women in this situation have to make is, as ever, what form of part-time childcare to choose. For those mothers who have employed childcarers before, this will probably mean a change in their arrangements (unless there are pre-school age children still at home) and necessitate a complete rethink about what is possible and desirable, both in terms of their children's development and the finances involved. For new working mothers, however, it will mean a survey of what is available and much agonising about what is going to be best for their children.

Because school cares for, stimulates and educates children between the hours of roughly 9am and 3.30pm, full-time working mothers with school-age children have to think about the hours which still need childcare attention. On a normal working day (shift-work excluded) this may include anything up to a couple of hours or so in the morning and anything upwards of two to three hours in the evening. Some more fortunate full-time working mothers may be able to take their children to school but still need assistance in the evening. It doesn't stop there, however, as school holidays – summer, Christmas, Easter and the three half terms – in addition to occasional days off, such as staff training for the teachers, illnesses and visits to the dentist, also need to be taken into account in this situation. While a working mother can ensure that her annual holidays coincide with her child's to a certain extent, unless she is a teacher it is unlikely that full coverage can be provided in this way. The childcare demands in this situation are, therefore, part-time, erratic and unlikely to fit in with the timetable of anybody on the general job market.

If the mother in question wants to ensure that her child

remains in his own home in out-of-school hours, there are very few realistic options available to her. It is clearly nonsensical to contemplate retaining or taking on a full-time nanny as this would be a waste both of money and expertise. A nanny-share with somebody, say, who only has one pre-school child to look after is, however, a possibility. A full-time mother's help might be an option if she spends the rest of her time on household chores but it is a relatively expensive form of out-of-school care. An au pair costs less and, in some ways, fulfils the same functions but comes with a different set of expectations which have to be accommodated (*see* 'The au pair option').

If caring in the home is not a primary consideration, however, then a childminder can be used as a means of taking children to and from school and looking after them in the holidays. You would have to find one who is prepared to work somewhat irregular hours and it is most likely that you would have to pay a retainer for some of the hours she is not being used. Some mothers are able to make arrangements with others with children in the same school so that between them they can cover the out-of-school hours in question. While this can work well it is inevitably a complex arrangement which requires numerous back-ups to make it workable.

Working mothers find many different ways of coping with their childcare needs in this situation, many of them quite complex and frequently involving a number of different arrangements through one week. Some days, for instance, granny may be able to pick up the child while, on others, the childminder or another mother may perform the same function. The question of stability for the child needs to be addressed and, as ever, a sense of familiarity and routine are essential components where the child's development is concerned.

*

As with all the forms of pre-school care already discussed, the diversity often present in out-of-school childcare is characteristic of the British situation in which the state plays a minimal role and in which mothers are left to make their own plans without much help from anyone else. The often ad hoc solutions which emerge signal the lack of a general level of provision for all school-age children who are in this position. Research shows, in fact, that, in Britain, one in five primary school children go home to an empty house, and that one in six are left to their own devices in the school holidays. This is clearly an unacceptable statistic.

Because of this lamentable situation there is much discussion on the part of groups campaigning for better childcare in this area (among them the Kids' Clubs Network) about the need for around 2,500 clubs in this country which would look after children after school and in the holidays. At present around 500 exist although they are very unevenly distributed (with very few in rural areas for instance) and very uneven in quality. Ideally these clubs should provide care and play facilities for any schoolchild in the local community, and some already do. They should pick children up from school, provide them with adequate food; call a register to make sure that nobody has gone missing; and ensure that all the children reach their homes safely. The emphasis upon play and care is significant as these centres are set up, not to act as continuations of school, but to allow children from a range of ages to play together in a safe environment. They provide space, professional supervision, stimulation, and security for children up to around six o'clock when they are met by a parent, or a designated person.

These after-school or 'latchkey' schemes are usually

situated in what are called closed sites (i.e. not playgrounds or parks), often community centres, church halls, youth centres or schools themselves. They are funded in a variety of ways, either by the local authority, whether through the Departments of Education, Social Services, or Recreation; by voluntary groups such as Gingerbread (an organisation set up to work specifically on behalf of one-parent families); or privately by a sponsor or a local employer. The fees they charge vary enormously but, as many are subsidised in one way or another, they are often only nominal. They can provide working parents with enormous peace of mind and they clearly play an important role in out-of-school childcare.

Parents can get information about the availability of such schemes in their neighbourhood through their local authority, school, library or directly through the Kids' Clubs Network which keeps a register of them. Following the Children Act of 1989 all schemes caring for children between five and seven have to be registered with the local authority which visits to ensure that all facilities are up to standard. The children to staff ratio should be eight to one under the age of eight, for example, and there should be enough space available to make sure that the five to seven-year-old group is not overwhelmed by the older children.

In Wandsworth, for example, there is, at the time of writing, an After School Care facility provided through the Education Department which caters for the age range three to eleven. It operates from Monday to Friday but only between the hours of 3.15pm to 6.00pm. The cost is from £24 a week for three to four year olds but this goes down to just £9 a week after the age of five. The scheme covers the borough and is based in schools. In addition supervised playground facilities are available for over-eights between May and October. This local authority scheme is supplemented by two community-run projects, one of which is the Arndale Community Project Latchkey Club which, for the price of £10.50 a week, provides up to 30 children with after-school care up to 6.00pm. This scheme picks up children from four schools in the neighbourhood and is open between 9.00am and 6.00pm during holidays. Clearly, Wandsworth is relatively well served in this context. While some other London boroughs are better served (covering longer hours for example), some have no after-school facilities at all, while others have a minimal structure in place. As ever, this sort of scheme is largely an urban phenomenon, and rural areas are relatively badly served.

Because the quality of the existing groups is somewhat uneven it is important to make sure that you visit one, with your child, before you enrol him in it. You need to reassure yourself that the atmosphere is friendly, relaxed, stimulating and safe and that your child will enjoy it there. Perhaps the greatest disadvantage of these schemes is that they tend to be based in institutions of different kinds and it is therefore difficult to create a homely atmosphere. This is compensated for by the level of stimulus, enjoyment and companionship that is on offer. Although children are usually tired after a day at school this kind of stimulus, if properly engineered, can make a child forget that he is tired and find new sources of energy within him. This is not a situation in which a tired child simply flops in front of a television set, as is often the case in the home, but rather, in the best schemes, one in which a weary child can be re-energised.

Having said that, it is clearly a difficult situation for the more introverted child as it demands him to play freely in a group of children covering a wide age range who are less well known to him than his immediate peers. Some children, indeed, need a couple of hours on their own after a day in a class full of other children. Each child needs to be considered individually before the right care formula for him can be finally decided upon.

Where working parents are concerned latchkey schemes have the restriction that hours are fixed and children have to be delivered and picked up promptly. This can be difficult when traffic flow and public transport are so unpredictable but, in contrast to workplace nurseries for pre-school age children, they provide a good community base for your child. He is very likely to have classmates alongside him at his playscheme and parents can become integrated more into their local community through their children attending such schemes. They can even share the task of picking the children up if that should prove practical.

It should be remembered that for older children the alternative to an after-school scheme may well be hanging around on street corners, playing in limited space at home, or playing outside near dangerous roads. Long gone are the days when children could play safely on their own in our urban environments, and these schemes provide safety as well as care for the children of working mothers.

Alternatives to this form of scheme, on which children are registered and a fee is paid, do exist but they are perhaps of less use to working parents as they do not provide the same degree of security. These alternatives are frequently situated on what are called open sites, that is, playgrounds and parks, and they usually operate on a 'come and go as you like' basis. As such they are clearly quite inappropriate for young school children. Local authority-funded playcentres do not set out to act *in loco parentis* but rather to be a form of organised play for children who wish to participate. No collection from school is provided with this arrangement and, indeed, they may well not even operate on a daily basis. Staff/children ratios tend to be lower than in after-school schemes and little more than a drink and biscuit (if there is any food at all) is usually provided.

The adventure playground idea grew up in the 1960s as a means of encouraging children who did not have much space at home to participate in communal free play. Again children are free to come and go as they wish. Increasingly snacks are provided in these places but playgrounds are not really suitable for the under-nines as they demand a great deal of independence from the children who use them and there are no registers of participants.

School holidays can be a nightmare for working parents. They might be able to find somebody in the local community who can pick up their child after school and give him tea until one parent can get home. They might even have a neighbour or relative who will cover for them for a day's illness, but the spectre of two whole weeks or more at Christmas and Easter, and the full six weeks or more in the summer, in addition to half terms, may seem an unresolvable problem. Partners juggle their own holidays to cover as much as possible but still the problem remains. Home-based arrangements such as mothers' helps and au pairs have to be given greater childcare, and fewer housework responsibilities at these times (although it can prove problematic where the latter's English lessons are concerned). It can also put an excessive strain on an otherwise effective nanny-share. Some mothers have arrangements with childminders which cover the holidays but others simply find that care is not easily available at these times.

The only options in this situation are the local authority and voluntary holiday playschemes, or private holiday schemes or activity holidays which may involve a child staying away from home for a period of time. Again some areas of the country have better provision in this context than others. A researcher who looked into the schemes available in Brighton in the summer of 1991, for instance, discovered that there were 22 schemes running in that town. While some were being run by the local authority, others were organised by voluntary charities, and others were run on an entirely private basis, albeit with grants from the local authority in certain instances.

At the time of writing Wandsworth runs a holiday playcentre scheme which sets out to provide a service for working parents, but which also recognises the importance of the nature of the care that children are receiving. For this service Wandsworth charges £10 a child for a week, or part of a week, or £20 for a family. Under certain circumstances those charges are waived. Parents are sent, via their child's school, a list of which schools will be providing playcentres and are asked to apply. Wandsworth is conscious of the need to reassure parents of their concern about the quality of the care in question and to this end has set out as the aims of its holiday playcentre scheme:

1. To provide a friendly, caring, safe and secure environment for young people.
2. To enhance the understanding and importance of play, language and social development through stimulating and structured play activities in a non-formal environment.
3. To encourage awareness of the social and environmental factors that influence a child's progress.
4. To create an environment for equal opportunities.

These criteria for quality are the ones outlined in the Children Act and should, indeed, underpin, all out-of-school care provided everywhere.

*

Providers of holiday playschemes other than local authorities and voluntary bodies, include employers, an increasing number of whom are beginning to realise that, like workplace nurseries, holiday playschemes are a vital strategy if they are to continue to recruit and retain women in their workforces. Employers who recognise that childcare does not stop at the age of five include the Midland Bank, the Civil Service and Boots.

Boots ran its first holiday playscheme in the summer of 1991. They used their sportsground at Trent Bridge as a base for a playcentre for the children aged five to fourteen of all their Nottingham-based staff. They recruited a team of six playworkers who were given two days' training by the Kids' Clubs Network which provides such a service as an encouragement for companies to develop initiatives such as this. They learnt about teamwork, first aid and fire safety. Toys and equipment were donated from within Boots and the playworkers devised a programme of on-site activities which included a drama workshop, T-shirt painting, a scavenger hunt, a monster afternoon and puppet-making, and outings which included swimming, den-making, a barbecue and a visit to the 'Tales of Robin Hood' theme centre. Lessons the company learnt from their first experiment included the fact that they had priced it too highly (they subsequently reduced it from £50 a week to £35 a week); that they needed to provide a transport system to and from their main site; and that, in order to attract older children, they needed to rename the project, 'The Boots Summer Activity Scheme'. As with nurseries, the relatively poor provision by the state in this area means that one looks to companies such as Boots to expand these kinds of facilities in the future.

Numerous other privately-run schemes exist, some run

on a daily basis, and others on a live-in basis. Many of the holiday-camp variety emphasise outdoor activities of all kinds while others are oriented to more creative activities, such as art and craft, ballet and drama. Many museums and art centres run courses of these kinds, especially in London and the larger urban centres. They can help occupy children during the long summer break when, even if there is a parent at home, they can be in need of extra stimulus and the companionship of children of their own age. This is especially true of only children. Increasingly such organisations are realising the important role that they are playing in helping working parents cope with the school holidays, and they timetable themselves accordingly wherever possible. Inevitably they need to be self-funding and have to charge prices which sometimes make them inaccessible to large numbers of families. Employer schemes, when they exist, such as that provided by Boots, however, are generally subsidised and so can often be offered on a cheaper basis.

All in all the out-of-school hours childcare situation is generally patchy and piecemeal. It cannot be discussed in the same way as pre-school childcare which is easier to think about, in some ways, because it is a full-time problem which has to be solved with full time answers and large sums of money. Out-of-school hours childcare is seasonal and part-time and so, on the one hand, is less of an economic proposition but, on the other, harder to grasp mentally. It is also a largely invisible problem as people tend to deal with it in a hand-to-mouth fashion rather than recognising it fully. It is also a non-static problem as different solutions present themselves as a child moves through different stages. While he may not, for example, want to attend an after-school scheme at the age of six, two years later he may be desperate to do so because his best friends go and he doesn't want to be left out.

Where children's development is concerned, it is clearly undesirable for them to spend all the hours of the day outside their home, and all their holidays away at a holiday camp. It is, of course, a question of balance and there is no harm in them being involved in organised play activity outside school hours, or in holiday schemes which prevent them being bored and introduce them to new activities, whether creative or sporting. Providing their 'centre of gravity' is a secure base within the home, and they have made the necessary emotional attachments to their primary carers at the right stage in their development, there should be no problems.

The question of over-stimulus is one to consider carefully in this context as children clearly need as much quiet, individual time as they do group stimulus, but this will, of course, vary from child to child and must be catered for as appropriate. As with nurseries, however, there is no evidence that quality care of the after-school kind does any developmental damage and it can at least provide a safe, secure environment for play. It also provides an important service for the working parent. No schemes will take children later than around 6.00pm so there is no danger of parents 'dumping' their children for an excessive amount of time, nor of children being left to play without some trained help being near at hand. The local authority supervision up to the age of eight is also an important safeguard on the situation. In these circumstances there is more chance of neglect, in fact, when the childcare is in the home and parents working very long hours use an au pair or a mother's help to act as 'stand-ins'.

The other question which relates to that of the school child and other care, concerns the role that working parents can, or cannot, play in connection with the school itself and its role in the local community. It is, of course, vital that the parents make every effort possible to be involved with the school. If they cannot either take or pick up the child then they must certainly try to get to open evenings, carol concerts and any other evening and weekend events which involve parents. This provides a sense, for the child, that his parents are interested in where he goes everyday and that he is therefore in their thoughts even if they can't be with him physically. Nothing is more disheartening to small school children than to feel that his parents have no interest in this place which for him is so important. It might also be worthwhile engineering one day off from work a term just so that you can stay in his class one day and help like his friends' parents do from time to time.

The guilt which becomes a way of life for the working mothers of pre-school children is not suddenly lifted from your shoulders when they start school. Rather than worrying about what is going on with your child/nanny, child/childminder or child/nursery situation you become anxious about whether or not you can perform adequately as the mother of a school child; whether your child will feel different or not because you work and his mates' mothers don't; and indeed whether you will be able to relate to the other mothers. Often two communities of mothers emerge – on the one hand, those who work, and, on the other, those who don't. The biggest problem is not actually meeting anybody and not, for example, discovering quickly enough whether the dynamics of a certain class are working to your child's advantage. A great deal of effort is involved in being a working parent of a school child and feeling that you are part of the community in which your child goes to school. After-school play schemes play a part in bringing together parents who share this level of guilt and who can benefit enormously simply by talking about it to each other.

Finally the question of whether care should be located inside or outside the home is a fundamental dilemma which lies once again at the heart of out-of-school care. While the latter is being provided, albeit to date only to a limited extent, by the idea of 'latchkey' schemes – whether funded by the state, voluntary bodies, or employers – the former is most conveniently provided by the au pair (financially speaking that is). This form of childcare, as has already been suggested, comes, however, with a number of specific conditions attached to it. It is to these that the last chapter will address itself.

The au pair option

Choosing an au pair

Taking on an au pair is, without doubt, to choose the cheapest form of home-based childcare available. As a result it is a fairly popular option. It is also, however, open to a great deal of exploitation, abuse and misunderstanding. Also, because it involves working with somebody with a different cultural background from yourself, and a first language almost certainly different from your own, it is a childcare arrangement which requires even more sensitivity and understanding than the others. Like them, however, when it works well, it is a rich, rewarding and mutually beneficial solution which can lead to life-long friendships.

It is important to remember from the outset that taking on an au pair is a very different kind of commitment from employing a nanny and on a number of different levels. For a start, the two people are involved in childcare for very different reasons. Unlike the latter who has already been discussed at length, the former is most probably seeing it as an opportunity to learn, or improve, a new language; to experience a family lifestyle which is different from her own; and to participate in, and learn about, a new culture. This may be undertaken to fill in a year between school and college; to provide a maturing experience after education; or simply as a means of filling in a period of otherwise uncommitted time in a stimulating way.

It is important that the motivation for someone coming to work as an au pair is fully understood at the outset as negative reasons, such as leaving behind an unsatisfactory family situation, can sometimes lead to problems. For the most part, though, this interlude is seen as a challenge by the young girl who is contemplating it. She arrives, therefore, full of enthusiasm and energy (as well as a few forebodings), ready to encounter changes, surprises, but above all excitement. Caring for your children represents, therefore, for most au pairs, a means to an end, rather than the heart of the experience she wants to confront. In this respect, where childcare is concerned, she is a very different phenomenon from nannies and childminders and should be treated as such.

At the time of writing the Home Office, the governmental body which has most to do with au pairs because they are usually foreigners entering this country, describes an au pair as a 'single person, aged between 17 and 21, with no dependents, who has come to Great Britain from a western European country or, alternatively, from Malta, Cyprus, Turkey, Czechoslovakia or Hungary'. People who conform to this set of conditions can enter Great Britain, to work as an au pair, for a period of up to two years without having to obtain a work permit. They can re-enter the country providing their total period of stay doesn't exceed this period. In 1991 the Home Office issued special permits to just under 8,000 girls. This did not, however, include the enormous number of au pairs who came from European Community countries who do not need special permission to do so. By far the greatest number to obtain Home Office permits came from Sweden.

The Home Office also issues guidelines concerning the conditions under which au pairs are expected to work.

THE AU PAIR OPTION

Again, at the time of writing, they are expected to work a maximum of 30 hours a week and to receive a minimum of £36 as pocket money each week. One day a week must be kept entirely free from work. These guidelines are intended to prevent a family requiring an au pair to do all the housework, look after the children all day and act as a general dog's body all at the same time. The Home Office has, however, no means of ensuring that the guidelines are followed (they almost certainly are not in every case) but they mean, nonetheless, that a family that wants to enter into this arrangement can get some idea about what is expected.

What the Home Office doesn't determine, however, is the basis upon which the au pair arrangement is founded. An understanding of this is vital if you are thinking of taking one on to help with your childcare. An au pair is not a trained, or even necessarily an experienced, childcarer and therefore it is unrealistic to have any expectations about her performance in this area. Neither is she coming to live in your house as an employee, but rather as a member of the family.

This last point is a fundamental one and it indicates a strong difference between an au pair and a live-in nanny. Whereas the latter enters your domestic sphere as a professional, employed to do a job and, at the same time, to share your living accommodation and enter into the family's private domain, an au pair enters your house, primarily, as a temporary member of the family unit. As a result she becomes a kind of older sister to the children and an older daughter to the parents, albeit for a limited period of time. This means that she will most probably eat with you, at least some of the time, and participate in family outings and holidays if she wishes to. Inevitably, however, it is likely that as she settles in and finds a group of friends in the community, her close integration into the family may weaken and she may well wish to spend more time outside the unit.

It is in not fully understanding this expectation of the au pair situation that many arrangements go wrong. A high level of responsibility exists on the part of the family that takes on the au pair to ensure that she enters British family life and settles into it in as happy and relaxed a way as possible. She will no doubt, also, want to attend English language classes and should certainly be both allowed and encouraged to do so. Her first reason for being in Britain, after all, is most probably to learn the language.

Au pairs and childcare

Where does childcare fit into this picture? The special characteristics of the au pair mean that it is very unlikely that she will be able to take on a sole charge role with a pre-school child for a number of reasons. While au pairs are seldom trained childcarers, many have, nonetheless, experience of looking after young children, whether their younger siblings or others, and may well be very good at it. Some may well, indeed, be more than capable of coping with young children on their own. This is, however, far from guaranteed and should not be expected.

Whatever a particular au pair's capabilities in this area there are other factors to take into consideration as well. The question of language is, of course, central and it may prove very difficult for your child to understand her. This clearly presents a problem and means that she cannot be left on her own with him for long stretches of time. It also presents difficulties when instructions are issued as you cannot be sure that they have been fully understood. This could be disastrous if, for instance, it involved not cooking chicken for long enough. Less seriously, it could be inconvenient if it involved, say, failing to pick the child up from somewhere at a fixed time. It is a hazard which does not exist with a nanny and should not be underestimated. In addition to the fact that an au pair is only expected to work a certain number of hours a day, which means that she could not be a childcarer for a full-time working mother, she probably also wants to attend a language school for part of the day so she could not act in this capacity anyway.

The most sensible way in which to use an au pair as a childcarer is when the child is at school and it is either pre or post-school care which is needed. In this situation an au pair who attends language classes (or simply 'does her own thing') in the afternoon might be asked to give a child his breakfast, prepare him for school and take him there, while one whose class is in the morning could meet a child from school, give him his tea and, possibly, bath him and put him to bed (depending on the age of the child). The daily allowance of working hours allows for either (although not both) of these possibilities and could well prove ideal in a situation in which working parents could themselves fill in the rest of the daily childcare requirements. The obvious benefits of involving an au pair in picking up a child from school is that the child returns to his own home and, if tired, can flop and relax while she makes him some tea. Some mothers are happier with this idea than with that of their child spending another two and a half hours out of the home. The relationship between the au pair and the child needs to be a quality one in this situation, however. Some rudimentary language learning can even go on in this situation.

This, then, is probably one of the best ways in which an

au pair could contribute to your childcare, although other scenarios certainly exist. Among them is the idea of the au pair acting as a help for a mother who works part-time and who may have a child in a nursery for part of the day. The permutations and combinations are numerous and the flexibility significant. Other possibilities include that of an au pair undertaking light nursery duties during her working period. Like the mother's help described earlier, the au pair can be used to lighten the number of chores around the house and generally make the burden of running a family and coping with a full-time job a little easier.

When taking children to school or picking them up is concerned, however, the au pair can, as has just been mentioned, play an important role. It means, for example that a child doesn't have either to be minded in somebody else's home, or participate in what might be seen as exhausting after-school activities. Some people feel strongly that children, especially young school children, need to come straight back to the security and relaxed environment of their own home after school because they are exhausted and need time either to relax, unwind or play with their own toys for a while. The child's home, they feel, is the place where the least number of pressures and a minimum amount of stimulus exist. It is a time, they feel, when he can return to base and be himself in familiar, secure surroundings. Having an au pair in the house can make this possible.

It is also important, however, to ensure that the au pair has an empathy with the child she is looking after in this situation. Language differences and a lack of experience with children can result in a minimal amount of communication between the two parties in question. It may, in the very worst circumstances, also be the case that the au pair even feels antipathetic towards, or intimidated by, children and looks upon being with them as little more than a necessary chore. In those disastrous circumstances the fact that the child is in his own house would not adequately compensate for the lack of quality care in the period after school and before the return of his parents.

While many au pairs perform their childcare role perfectly well, and plenty of children enjoy being met from school by this new 'big sister' with a funny accent who makes unusual things for tea, in some cases the chemistry between the au pair and child is just not there. There is certainly no guarantee that the chemistry will work and parents should remain observant and sensitive to this potential situation.

Finding an au pair

There is a higher level of risk involved in finding a suitable au pair than in searching for a nanny or a childminder. In the latter two instances face-to-face interviews play a vital role in the parties involved not only being able to match their requirements but also feeling that they are dealing with somebody with whom they feel comfortable. It is uncommon, however, for a family and an au pair to meet before they are thrown together into the same domestic environment.

Ways of finding an au pair vary as widely as those of finding all the other forms of childcare outlined in this book. Agencies abound which will put you in contact with someone appropriate. As always they operate in a multitude of different ways but most specialise in girls from particular countries. They have agencies in the countries where the initial contact is made which supply details about the girls in question to the British agency. A client is usually provided with a letter from the potential au pair, a photograph and two references. They can talk to them by telephone or simply ask the agency to act on their behalf and approach the girl they have selected. As a result the contact will be made and the details of arriving and starting work are arranged to mutual convenience.

In addition to providing this service agencies also act as a protective filter to the au pairs on their books inasmuch as they outline the Home Office requirements to their clients. They also often help in creating a support network for au pairs in their area in the form of, say, sending them copies of *Au Pair* magazine and letting them know when local au pair coffee mornings are taking place. They also explain to their clients the conditions involved in taking on au pair like, for instance, the fact that the family is expected to help the au pair enrol in a language class and pay for transportation to and from it (au pairs are generally expected to pay their own fees, in addition to their travel to and from Great Britain, although circumstances vary in different arrangements), and how many evenings they can expect the au pair to babysit for them a week (sometimes as many as three!). Agencies also remind clients that au pairs need a room to themselves and that they like to eat with the family for the most part and be involved in family activities. Housework done by au pairs, they emphasise, should be light and they stress that one day of the week must be kept free from work.

The main problem, however, in being put in touch with an au pair through an agency is that agreements are usually made on a completely 'unseen' basis. Neither party has more than telephone contact with the other and the potential au pair does not even have the advantage of seeing a photograph or taking up references. An agency's recommendation in this instance is everything. On the basis of that alone a girl will buy an air-ticket, leave her family and country, and turn up to be met in a foreign land by a complete stranger with whom she will be living from that moment onwards. It takes a high level of courage to enter into this arrangement and the au pair is in a very vulnerable position. In many ways, it's not surprising that one hears as many horror stories as one does (especially bearing in mind the low cost of an au pair).

This is not to say, however, that very many good arrangements do not also result from a family/au pair relationship brought about through the mediation of an agency, because there are, of course, many. Some people are able to avoid the risks which are unavoidable when you go through an agency by finding an au pair on the basis of a recommendation. This may be from a previous au pair who is in a good position to 'match-make', or from a friend or acquaintance who lives abroad and who knows the family of the girl in question. Inevitably the best form of introduction is through somebody who knows both parties well and is confident that the relationship will work. Many au pairing positions are found through such networks of people and often work out very well.

Another means of procuring an au pair is to advertise, and once again *The Lady* plays a prominent role here as several of its pages are filled with such advertisements. Once again, the closest contact both parties will have with each other before committing themselves is likely to be a phone call or an exchange of letters. The protective role of the agency is also missing in this situation and the au pair is consequently very much on her own when she takes up her position.

The daily routine

It will inevitably take a little longer to settle an au pair into a routine than it does with a nanny. First she has to get used to a new country, sign up for her language classes, and generally begin to feel at home. One should not underestimate the fact that she is young, often quite immature, and not necessarily used to being away from her family and friends. There are two schools of thought regarding whether or not the host family should speak to the au pair in her mother tongue (if indeed it is able to) but it seems sensible, in the first instance, to use it just long enough for her to begin to be confident about speaking some English. Where a child is involved this is unlikely to be possible so the sooner she can speak English to him the better. Many au pairs find, though, that they communicate more easily with young children whose language is still relatively unsophisticated. It is of little harm for the child to get a smattering of a second language, however, should the au pair sometimes speak to him in her own language.

For a small child this introduction to a new language and culture forms, in fact, the basis of a strong argument for the use of au pairs in childcare. A number of people feel that this is the ideal way in which to introduce a young child to a new language as he is confronting it in his own home and is therefore not intimidated by it. Indeed there are instances of families in which one parent has a non-English first language, but doesn't have time to teach it to his child, and therefore uses the au pair option as a means of introducing it to him. It goes beyond a question of language alone, however, into all the manifestations of a different culture, whether it be types of cooking, everyday rituals or even ways of dressing. All of this can be a highly enriching experience for a young child, and often one which will remain with him longterm.

A good deal of help should be given to your au pair in the early days of your partnership. She has to be introduced to the neighbourhood, to the child's school, park, friends, to the daily routine, and to the language school she will attend. All this takes time and the host family has to exert a considerable amount of effort in the first few days to ensure that she is accepted into the community, especially by other mothers, nannies and au pairs, before she is thrown into her childcare role on a regular basis. All too often au pairs remain marginal in the playground situation and this, in turn, can marginalise the child she is looking after as well.

In addition to everything concerning the au pair's conditions of service, the childcare role she will be expected to play and the housework she will be asked to do must be clarified before she starts work. It is vital that this is not only explained but that the family makes sure that it has been fully understood. This can be a frustrating and exhausting task but it will reap rewards later. It is very easy to think that an au pair has understood something only to find later that she hasn't. Common sense, patience and kindness coupled with a degree of firmness are essential in these early days. As with all kinds of childcarers it is also important to express worries and problems as they come along rather than to wait until they become traumas. As communication is one of the most sensitive areas in the au pair/working parent relationship, and time is always at a premium, it needs to be given extra attention if misunderstandings are to be avoided.

One should not underestimate, also, how tiring the first few weeks of living in a new country and speaking a new language can be. It is unfair, and unwise, therefore, to expect an au pair to become a member of the household as quickly as a trained nanny. She will take time to feel at home and cannot be rushed. If you speak her language there is, as has been mentioned, an argument for using it a little in the first few days simply while she acclimatises herself. Beyond that, of course, it must be back to English as that is why she came to Britain. If you don't speak her language then you simply have to expect a settling-in period to elapse before you even know whether the arrangement is going to work or not.

Some people take their au pairs away with them at weekends and on holiday. Given that part of the reason for her being here is to get to know another culture she will probably be eager to see something of the country other than your immediate location. Alternatively she may find that she would rather do this in the company of new-found friends of her own age; with you she may feel that it is difficult to move out of the 'on duty' mode.

Perhaps the most difficult thing for an au pair to feel part of is school playground culture, which is a complex one at the best of times. She will probably be younger than a good many of the mothers picking up their children, and will certainly feel very distant from them in a multitude of ways. As a result it can be a problem to get any of the playground gossip through au pairs or even to be sure that all messages from school get back home. Childminders and nannies can penetrate this network more easily and their help can be drawn on to introduce the au pair to the new situation. However, they all belong to different cliques and in the end the au pair is probably going to feel closest to another au pair.

If an au pair picks up your child from school you also have to think about what will happen when childhood illnesses strike, or indeed when she is ill herself. Half-terms and holidays also need to be thought through carefully as they may not necessarily coincide exactly with her language school breaks. Also she may want to go on all-day trips with the school when they are arranged. The au pair is unlikely to want to miss her language class and, indeed, should not be expected to as a matter of principle. These matters must be discussed in the early days of the arrangement. It may be that your au pair will feel it part of her childcare duty to take time off when the child is ill. If not, one is back to relatives, neighbours or a day off work. None of these arrangements are foolproof and illness can disrupt the most smoothly running arrangements. With an au pair individual girls will have different expectations of their role but, in principle, they are here for their own reasons and should not be expected to act as mother substitutes.

In the end the au pair is, in many ways, the perfect solution for the working mother with a child at school who wants that child to be in his own home as much as possible, or who simply wants him to have a gentle introduction to another language or culture. It is an arrangement which demands a lot of give and take, especially on the part of the working mother, and it cannot be expected to be a solution to all the childcare needs which will arise in this situation. Often, however, an au pair proves to be the ideal childcarer and is only too willing to help out in emergencies as repayment for the kindness and hospitality that she has been shown. This is when the arrangement works best and it should be striven for, however tiring and demanding it may seem at times.

Conclusion

The most recurrent theme in this discussion of childcare options in Britain in the 1990s has been the complexity and diversity of the existing situation, and the need for enormous care when setting out to assess it. Each individual working mother has to take this complexity on board if she is to decide what will be right for her and for her child. There are no short cuts and no formulae for success – this is a world with no absolutes, other than that of the highest possible quality in the option selected from the choices available at any one time.

Both the diversity and the emotional nature of the world of childcare are peculiar to the British experience in many ways. The fact that we can choose between nannies, childminders, a wide variety of types of nurseries, or countless combinations and permutations of these, is a direct result of the lack of state intervention in this area and the absence of the state-run nursery system which is so widespread in much of the rest of Europe. A much more open-minded approach towards mothers in the workforce exists in those countries, a fact supported by a comparison of the numbers of mothers returning to full-time work in a few of them. While, for example, four out of ten do so in France, the figure is eight out of ten in Sweden, but only two or three in Britain. This is a reflection both of attitudes and of practicalities.

In Sweden, for example, mothers not only have much more maternity leave than us – 450 days in fact – they also have a widespread system of state-run nurseries in which they can put their babies from the very early months right up to school age, should they wish to return to work earlier than this. This is the case in all the Scandinavian countries. The level of maternal guilt is thus reduced, and the level of governmental monitoring of, and public enthusiasm for, the idea of the pre-school nursery is much higher than it is here. There are signs in these countries, also, however, that demand is beginning to outstrip supply, and a private, profit-oriented system is beginning to fill the gap, but there is nothing, as yet, on the scale that there is in Britain.

The fact that the state plays such a low profile in this area in Britain, and that there is so little subsidy in general, whether public or from private companies, throws the financial responsibility of childcare firmly on to the shoulders of the private individual. Choice becomes, therefore, as we have seen through the pages of this book, largely, although not exclusively, a question of finances, and there can be little doubt that many women are prevented from going back to work in this country simply because they cannot afford to do so.

The absence of a state-run and funded system of childcare also means that we have to fall back, in Britain, on to old models of carers, and the nanny and the minder are good examples of history providing us with childcare 'types', however much they are being redefined in our ever changing society. Clearly, however, if these models are the ones which will remain with us into the next century, then a few changes need to be made, among them the removal of double taxation for working parents who employ nannies (an anomaly which has been given very little attention to date), and the provision of a stronger back-up system for childminders who are often working with little support from their local communities.

There are clearly political and cultural issues which arise from examining the nature of childcare for working parents in this country, and hopefully they will be addressed in some way in the next decade. However, the greatest hope for improvement in this area lies in the hands of the consumers themselves, that is, those working parents who are going to continue to make demands of the system, and who are going to need quality childcare of all kinds in the years ahead. There are signs that the pressure groups are becoming more and more vociferous and, at least where the media is concerned, signs that their voices are being heard.

As in so many areas of life in Britain in the 1990s, be it equal opportunities, health, education, or the environment, it seems that the strongest ripples are coming from below, and that it is today's movements of consumers, and their opinions, which are stimulating the most significant changes within contemporary society. This seems to be beginning to happen in the area of childcare for working parents, also, as the people for whom it is so vital begin to flex their muscles.

I hope, therefore, that this book will not only help its readers to make more informed and intelligent choices about the kind of care that they choose for their children, and feel more confident about making those choices, but that it will also play a part, however small, in the enormous groundswell of popular feeling about the need for reform in the system of childcare provided for working parents in Britain in the 1990s.

Bibliography

Beard, M. *The Good Working Mother's Guide* Duckworths (London, 1989)

Binswanger, B. and Ryan, B. *Live-in Childcare* Dolphin, Doubleday and Co. (New York, 1986)

Blackstone, T. *A Fair Start: the provision of pre-school education* Penguin (Harmondsworth, 1971)

Bone, M. *Pre-School Children and the Need for Daycare* HMSO (London, 1977)

Brannen, J. and Moss, P. *New Mothers at Work: Employment and Childcare* Unwin (London, 1988)

Breese, C. and Gomer, H. *The Good Nanny Guide* Century Hutchinson (London, 1988)

Cohen, B. *Caring for Children. Services and Policies for Childcare and Equal Opportunities in the UK* Report for the European Commission's European Childcare Network. Commission of European Communities (1988, 1990)

Cohen, B. and Clarke, K. (eds) *Childcare and Equal Opportunities: Some Policy Perspectives* Equal Opportunities Commission HMSO (London, 1986)

Cullum, M. *Becoming a Nursery Nurse* Batsford (London, 1986)

Cuthbert, A. and Holford, A. *The Briefcase and the Baby: A Nanny and Mother's Handbook* Mandarin (London, 1992)

Daniel, W. *Maternity Rights: The Experience of Women* Policy Studies Institute (London, 1980)

Dix, C. *Working Mothers* Unwin (London, 1989)

Employer's guide to Childcare The Working Mothers Association (London, 1991)

Femiola, C. *Day Care in the Home: A Report* Working for Children in Wandsworth (London, 1992)

Finch, S. and Morgan, D. *Childcare in the Balance: A Discussion on Childcare and Taxation in the UK* Working for Childcare (London, 1991)

Gathorne-Hardy, J. *The Rise and Fall of the British Nanny* Weidenfeld and Nicholson (London, 1972)

Hennessey, E., Martin, S., Moss, P., and Melhuish, E. *Children and Day Care: Lessons from Research* Paul Chapman Publishing (London, 1992)

Hogg, C. *Under Five and Under Funded* Daycare Trust (London, 1988)

Hogg, C. and Harker, L. *The Family-Friendly Employer: Examples from Europe* Daycare Trust (London, 1992)

Hodgkinson, L. *The Working Woman's Guide* Thorsons Publishers (London, 1985)

Holterman, S. *The Costs of Caring* National Children Bureau (London, 1992)

Katz, A. *The Juggling Act* Bloomsbury (London, 1992)

Kozak, M. (ed) *Daycare for Kids: A Parents' Survival Guide* Daycare Trust (London, 1989)

Joshi, H. 'The Cost of Caring' in Glendenning, C. and Miller, C. (eds) *Women and Poverty in Britain* Wheatsheaf (Brighton, 1987)

Leira, A. *Daycare for Children in Denmark, Norway and Sweden* Institute for Social Research (Oslo, 1987)

McRae, S. and Daniel, W.W. *Maternity Rights in Britain: The Experience of Women and Employers* First Findings, Policy Studies Institute (London, 1991)

Martin, J. and Roberts, C. *Women and Employment: A Lifetime Perspective* HMSO (1984)

Mayall, B. and Petrie, P. *Childminding and Day Nurseries – What kind of Care?* Heinemann (London, 1983)

Meeting the Childcare Challenge: Can the Market Provide? Working for Childcare (London, 1990)

Melhuish, E.C. and Moss, P. *Day Care for Young Children: International Perspectives* Routledge (London, 1991)

Michaels, M. (ed) *The ABC of Quality Childcare* Daycare Trust (London, 1991)

Morgan, P. *The Hidden Costs of Childcare* Family Education Trust (London, 1992)

Moss, P. *A Review of Childminding Research* Thomas Coram Research Unit (London, 1987)

Moss, P. *Childcare and Equality of Opportunity: Consolidated Report to the European Commission* Commission of the European Communities (Brussels, 1988)

Moss, P. *Childcare in the Early Months: How Childcare Arrangements are Made for Babies* Occasional Paper 3 Thomas Coram Research Unit (London, 1989)

Moss, P. and Brannen, J. *Managing Mothers* Unwin Hyman (London, 1990)

Moss, P. and Melhuish, E (eds) *Current Issues in Day Care for Young Children* Department of Health HMSO (London, 1990)

Mottershead, P. *Evaluation of Recent Initiatives in Childcare* HMSO (London, 1990)

Mottershead, P. *Recent Developments in Childcare: A Review* HMSO (London, 1988)

Mottershead, P. *Setting Up a Workplace Nursery: A Manual for Employers and Employees* Equal Opportunities Commission (London, 1979)

New, C. and David, M. *For the Children's Sake: Making Childcare more than Women's Business* Penguin (Harmondsworth, 1985)

Oakley, A. *From Here to Maternity: Becoming a Mother* Penguin (Harmondsworth, 1979)

Petrie, P. and Logan, P. *After School and in the School Holidays* Thomas Coram Research Unit (London, 1987)

Phillips, A. *Until They are Five: A Parent's Guide* Pandora (London, 1989)

Sanger, S. MD. and Kelly, J. *The Woman Who Works, the Parent Who Cares* Corgi (London, 1990)

Scarr, S. and Dunn, J. *Mother Care, Other Care: The Childcare Dilemma for Women and Children* Penguin (Harmondsworth, 1987)

Sharpe, S. *Double identity: the lives of working mothers* Penguin (Harmondsworth, 1984)

Slaughter, E. (ed) *The Working Woman's Handbook* Century (London, 1986)

Solomon, J. *Holding the Reins* Fontana (London, 1987)

So You Want to Find a Childminder? National Childminding Association (London, 1988)

Social Affairs Unit, *Families in Dreamland* (London, 1992)

Statham, J., Lloyd, E., Moss, P., Melhuish, E., and Owen, C. *Playgroups in a Changing World* Department of Health HMSO (London, 1990)

The Working Parents' Handbook The Working Mothers Association (London, 1991)

Thompson, M. *A Handbook for Nannies* Batsford (London, 1986)

Velmans, M. and Litvinoff, S. *Working Mother: A Practical Handbook* Corgi (London, 1987)

Childcare Now
The Quarterly Magazine of the Daycare Trust and the National Childcare Campaign

Useful addresses

Many of the organisations listed here have regional groups and branches, the addresses of which can be obtained from their headquarters.

Central Bureau for Educational Visits and Exchanges
Seymour Mews
London W1H 9PE
Tel: 071 486 5101

The Childcare Association
8 Talbot Road
London N6 4QR

The Federation of Recruitment and Employment Services
(for nanny and au pair agencies)
36–38 Mortimer Street
London W1N 7RB
Tel: 071 323 4300 & 071 235 6616

Gingerbread
35 Wellington Street
London WC2E 7BN
Tel: 071 240 0953

The Home Office
Immigration and Nationality Department
Lunar House, 40 Wellesley Road
Croydon CR9 2BY
Tel: 081 760 1417

Kids' Clubs Network
279–281 Whitechapel Road
London E1 1BY
Tel: 071 247 3009

The Lady
39–40 Bedford Street
London WC2E 9ER

London Montessori Centre
18 Balderton Street
London WIY 1TG
Tel: 071 493 0165

The Maternity Alliance
15 Britannia Street
London WC1X 9JP
Tel: 071 837 1265

Nannies Incorporated
63–64 Margaret Street
London W1N 7FJ
Tel: 071 323 3338

Nannies Need Nannies
28 May Street
South Shields
Tyne and Wear NE 33 3AJ

The National Association of Certified Nursery Nurses
162 Langdale Road
Thornton Heath
Surrey CR4 7PR

National Childbirth Trust
Alexander House
Oldham Terrace
Acton
London W3 6NH
Tel: 081 992 8637

National Childcare Campaign/Daycare Trust
Wesley House
4 Wild Court
London WC2B 5AU
Tel: 071 405 5617

National Childcare Directory
1 Ickleton Road
Wantage
Oxford OX12 9EX

National Childminding Association
8 Masons Hill
Bromley
Kent BR2 9EX
Tel: 081 464 6164

National Children's Bureau
8 Wakeley Street
Islington
London EC1V 7QE
Tel: 071 278 9441

National Children's Play and Recreation Unit
First floor
359–361 Euston Road
London NW1 3AL
Tel: 071 383 5455

National Council for One-Parent Families
255 Kentish Town Road
London NW5 2LX
Tel: 071 267 1361

The National Council of Voluntary Childcare Organisations
Cheriton Barton
Cheriton Fitzpaine
Crediton, Devon EX17 4JB

National Nursery Examination Board
8 Chequer Street
St Albans
Herts AL1 3XZ
Tel: 0727 47636

National Toy Libraries Association
68 Church Way
London NW1 1LT
Tel: 071 387 9592

Network Nannies
(an agency for nannies who want to work with handicapped children)
22 Chelsham Road
Clapham
London SW4 6NP

New Ways to Work
309 Upper Street
London N1 2TY
Tel: 071 224 2401

Nursery World
The School House Workshop
51 Calthorpe Street
London WC1X 0HH
Tel: 071 837 7224

Pre-School Playgroups Association
61–63 Kings Cross Road
London WC1X 9LL
Tel: 071 833 0991

The Professional Association of Nursery Nurses (PANN)
2 St James' Court
Friar Gate
Derby DE1 1BT
Tel: 0332 43029

Thomas Coram Foundation for Children
40 Brunswick Square
London WC1N 1AZ
Tel: 071 278 2424

Working Mothers Association
77 Holloway Road
London N7 8JZ
Tel: 071 700 5771

Working for Childcare
77 Holloway Road
London N7 8JZ
Tel: 071 700 0281

Workplace Nurseries Campaign
Room 205
Southbank House
Black Prince Road
London SE1 7SJ

Index

Adventure playgrounds, 170
Agencies, professional, 36–7, 42, 86
Aristocracy, and child-upbringing, 13–14, 19
Au pairs: and childcare, 180–3; choosing, 177–80; contrasted with nannies, 179; daily routine, 186–9; finding, 183; Home Office and, 178–9, 184; reasons for being, 177–8; settling in, 187–8; status in family, 179–80
Australia, 91
Authority, maintaining joint, 61–4

Babies: care of, 30; lack of daycare for, 130–2; new, 78–9, 89; and working mothers, 28
Babies in Daycare (Kodak), 138
Baby-sitting, 66
Back-up, emergency, *see* Emergency
Backing up decisions, 61
Bath- and bed-time, 54–5
Box numbers, 38
Brannen, J., and Moss, P., 115–16, 122
Breastfeeding, 113, 146

Brighton, 171

Careers: breaks in, 163–4; pursuit of, 21; *see also* Mothers, returning to work
Cars, access to, 46
Child-bearing age, 16
Childcare: at home or elsewhere?, 17, 97–8, 176; lack of state provision, 17–18, 124, 129–30, 142, 152, 190; old-style, 20; professional, 21; qualifications, 21–3; quality of, 3–6; statistics, 130; those offering experience, *see* Childminders; those offering training, *see* Nannies; types, popularity compared, 130; ways into professional, 21
Childminders: 8, 18, 86, 89, 165; advantages, 103–4; and children's group dynamics, 122; cost of, 99; 'culture' of, 118; finding, 108; flexibility lacking with, 104–6, 117, 118, 123; friction, potential for, 120–5; function, 124; groups of, 117–18; and illness, 123–4, 136; interviewing, 108–12; and

the law, 96, 108, 122;
limitations, 104–7; mother's
lack of control over, 120–1;
mother's relationships with,
106–7, 114–16, 122–4;
motives for being, 101, 112;
motives for employing, 95–6;
or nannies?, 100–3;
negotiating terms with,
112–14; numbers of, 95;
perceptions of, 101–2;
routine, establishing a,
116–19; standards required
of, 124–5; statutory
requirements, 96–7.
Children: at interviews, 109; at
risk, 141; development and
upbringing, 4–6, 67–8, 70–1,
104, 111, 139, 174; as
manipulators, 48, 53–4,
62–3; second, 18; social life
of, 51–3, 77–8, 80, 106, 122,
147; *see also* Babies;
Under-fives
Children Act, 1989:, 7, 133, 144,
167, 171
Class differences, 115–16
Clients, mothers as, 115, 120, 124
'Come-and-go-as-you-like'
schemes, 169–70
Community (voluntary) nurseries,
143–5; advantages, 145
Companies providing childcare,
148–51, 172
Confidentiality, 88
Conservative party, 17–18, 124,
129–30, 142, 152, 190
Contracts, employment, 41–6,
112–13
Corporal punishment, 70, 133
Costs, nannies/childminders,
99–100
Council nurseries, 140–2; entry
qualifications, 141;
inspected, 141; regional
variations, 142
Crèches, 158

Day nurseries: advantages, 136;
facilities, 132; fees, 135–6,
157–8; flexibility lacking
with, 134–5; introducing
children to, 137; law and
recommendations, 132–3; as
learning centres, 154–5;
opening hours and location,
133–4; popularity of, 130;
shortage of, 139; standards
of, 129; variety among, 157;
see also Private day nurseries
Daycare Trust, 152
Diet, 68
Disagreements, resolving, 66
Disciplining, of child, 69–70; of
employee, 45
Divorce, 18
Domesticity, cult of, 14, 98

Elitism, 130
Emergency back-up, 47, 74–5,
104, 136
Empathy with child, 182–3
Employers providing childcare,
148–51, 172
English language classes, 180,
184, 188–9
Europe, 3, 129, 140, 142, 190
Extended family, 57

Foreign languages, 186, 188
France, 190

Gathorne-Hardy, Jonathan,
13–14
Gingerbread, 167
Grandparents, 66, 165
Grievances, 45
Guilt feelings, *see under* Mothers

INDEX

Handing over to childcarer, 48–9, 117
Health insurance, 31
'Hidden' labour, 7, 29
Holiday camp-style schemes, 172–3
Holidays, 44, 75–7, 100, 113, 134–5
Home, childcare at, or elsewhere?, 97–8
'Home', concept of, 98
Hopkins, Juliet, 58
Humour, 56

Illness: childminders and, 123–4, 136; children's, 73–4, 123–4, 136, 188–9; nannies and, 44, 73–5
Insurance schemes, 31, 44, 112; *see also* National Insurance
Interviews, 39–41, 108–12
Introverted children, 138, 168

Jealousy, mother/nanny, 58–60, 71

Kids' Clubs Network, 166, 167, 172
Kodak, Marion, 138

Lady, The, 37, 82, 185
Language development, 111
Language/communication problems, 180–1
'Latchkey' children, 166–70
Live-in carers, advantages, 33–4
Local authorities, 29, 90, 96, 111, 112, 132, 140, 154; *see also* Council nurseries
Local knowledge, obtaining, 103
Local papers, 38
London: Battersea, 117–18; Haringey, 143; Lambeth, 37, 82, 150, 185; Lewisham, 144; Wandsworth, 130–1, 134, 155–6, 167–8, 171–2

Manners, teaching, 67–8
Maternity leave, paid, 27, 44, 191
Maternity nurses, 30–2
Mealtimes, live-in childcarers and, 46
Means-testing, 141
Middle classes, 14, 16, 17; upper, 13–14
Montessori system, 154–5
Mothers: anxiety, 58; arriving home, 54, 63; and children's safety, 54; guilt feelings and their effects, 18, 35, 48, 60–1, 69, 121, 142, 175, 191; ill, 74; leaving for work, 48–9; nannies, relationships with, 56–60, 71; returning to work after birth, 21, 27–8, 78–9, 190; tasks compared with nannies', 50–1; working, 1–10, 16
Mothers' helps, 90–1; defined, 91

Nannies: 7, 13–14, 17; authority, undermining of, 61–4; career structure, 81; changeover of, 80–3; or childminders?, 100–3; contracts with, 41–6; cost of, 99; 'culture' of, 47, 51–2, 80, 118; financing, 34–5; free hand for new, 47–9; friction, potential for, 62–72; and holidays, 44, 75–7; hours of work, 44; and illness, 44, 73–5; interviewing, 39–41; length of stay, 81; live-out, 35, 38, 84–5; and local mothers, 52–3; looking for, 36–9; and maternity/nursery nurses, 31; motives for being, 101;

motives for employing, 33–6; and new babies, 78–9; perceptions of, 101–2; relationships within household, 49–50, 56–72; rise in numbers, 29; rooms for, 36; routine, establishing, 47–9; sharing, *see* Shared nannies; structure of day, 49–55; tasks compared with mothers', 50–1; *see also* Jealousy

National Childbirth Trust, 18, 52, 86

National Childminding Association, 97

National Insurance, 42, 74, 88, 99

New Zealand, 91

NNEB (Nursery Nurse Examination Board), 21–2, 132, 135

Notice, giving, 45

Nottingham, 172

Nurseries: 95; changing concept of, 158–9; *see also* Community; Council; Day nurseries; Nursery schools; Private day nurseries; Workplace

Nursery nurses, 21–4; examining board, 21–2, 132, 135; professional body, 23–4

Nursery schools, publicly-funded, 158

Nursery World, 37

Opportunity 2000:, 2

Out-of-school care, 163–76; for child at home, 164–5; hours when needed, 164; overview, 173–4

PANN (Professional Association of Nursery Nurses), 23–4

Parents: away from home, 65; self-help, 143; *see also* Mothers

Part-time care, 156, 158; *see also* Out-of-school care; Shared nannies

Parties, organising, 77

Playcentres, 169–70

Playgroups, 134

Playschemes, 171–3

Poorer people, *see* Underprivileged

Pre-School Playgroups Association, 134

Private day nurseries, 153–7; regimes, sample, 155–6

Private/public divide, bridging, 143

Professional classes, 15

References, character, 39–40, 41

Registers, local authority, 29, 90, 96, 111, 132

Relatives, 18, 66, 165

Retainer fees, 165

Rossan, Dr Sheila, 58

School: holidays, 170–3; parents' involvement, 174–5; playground culture, 188; starting, 79–80

School-leavers, 91

Self-help, *see* Community nurseries

'Servant', concept of, 34

Shared nannies, 85–90; complications of, 87–8; finding, 86–7; multi-household, 89–90; pros and cons of, 88–90; resident or non-resident?, 88

Shared nurturing, 56–7

Sheffield, 144

INDEX

Social attitudes survey, 3
Social Services, 123–4, 130–1, 132, 140–1, 154, 155
SRNs (State Registered Nurses), 31
Staffing ratios, 96, 131, 136–8, 167, 170
Subsidised care, 140, 143, 148–51, 167, 169, 191
Sweden, 190–1

Tax, incentives, 149; payment, 42, 88, 99, 152, 191
Television-watching, 68–9
Terms of service, *see* Contracts
Toy libraries, 117

Under-fives, 118; provision for, *see* Nurseries

Underprivileged, the, 14, 18, 142, 144
United front before child, 62

Values, differing, 67–8, 111
Voluntary nurseries, *see* Community

Women: aspirations, 15; Employment Survey, 29; liberation movement, 15; *see also* Mothers
Working from home, problems of, 64–5
Working Mothers' Association, 2, 18, 42, 86, 152
Workplace nurseries, 133, 146–52; campaign, 152; pros and cons of, 146–8, 151–2

BRIGHT AS A BUTTON

Dr Joan Freeman

The world needs children that are as bright as buttons, who will develop their potential and contribute greatly to life. At least one in every ten children, millions around the world, is born clever enough to make him or her outstanding in some way.

This book is packed with ideas on how to make your home a learning centre that is a pleasure for a child to learn from. It tells you how to get the best for your child in whatever circumstances you live in, and how to keep on getting the best from what school has to give. It is concerned with children growing up, developing their talents and feelings, and learning how to be competent in society.

A parent, teacher and psychologist, Dr Joan Freeman is currently president of the European Council of High Ability. She has written this book primarily for parents to enable them to understand and help their children do their best and be happy, believing parents to be the best resource bright children have, since they are most sensitive to their needs and concerned about their future.

DOES MY CHILD NEED HELP?

J. Melville and Dr F. Subotsky

- Do my toddler's tantrums indicate a serious disturbance?

- Why is my child not progressing at school?

- Is my teenager's behaviour delinquent?

- Where can I find help?

This book provides a guide to common child/teenage behavioural problems and offers practical solutions, coping strategies, and clear advice on where professional help is recommended. An explanation of what the help entails is included.

The book also incorporates invaluable psychological insights into how many children's problems can be overcome and overall family relationships improved.

A GUIDE TO ADOPTION: THE OTHER ROAD TO PARENTHOOD

Deborah Fowler

In this book Deborah Fowler explores every aspect of the subject of adoption. For anyone – prospective adoptive parents, natural parents who have or are thinking of giving up their child for adoption, or adopted children themselves – this book is a must. The subjects covered include:

* who can adopt
* legal requirements
* financial
* emotional problems
* finding a child
* inter country adoption
* disabled children
* older children
* inter racial adoption

Many and varied are the types of people who would make wonderful adoptive parents yet perhaps do not recognise it. Using case histories to help illustrate the pros and cons, the author (who has adopted a Romanian baby herself) shows the way forward to those thinking of adoption.

[ ] BRIGHT AS A BUTTON by Joan Freeman £6.99
[ ] DOES MY CHILD NEED HELP?
    by J. Melville & Dr F. Subotsky £4.99
[ ] A GUIDE TO ADOPTION by Deborah Fowler £6.99

Optima Books now offers an exciting range of quality titles by both established and new authors which can be ordered from the following address:

Little, Brown and Company (UK) Limited,
P.O. Box 11,
Falmouth,
Cornwall TR10 9EN.

Alternatively you may fax your order to the above address.
Fax No. 0326 376423.

Payments can be made as follows: cheque, postal order (payable to Little, Brown and Company) or by credit cards, Visa/Access. Do not send cash or currency. UK customers and B.F.P.O. please allow £1.00 for postage and packing for the first book, plus 50p for the second book, plus 30p for each additional book up to a maximum charge of £3.00 (7 books plus).

Overseas customers including Ireland please allow £2.00 for the first book plus £1.00 for the second book, plus 50p for each additional book.

NAME (Block Letters) ....

....

ADDRESS ....

....

....

☐ I enclose my remittance for ....

☐ I wish to pay by Access/Visa Card
   Number ....
   Card Expiry Date ....